Menachem Begin Remembered

Hart N. Hasten

with

Peter Weisz

Brotchin Books

Published by **Brotchin Books,** an imprint of:

Peter Weisz Publishing, LLC
7143 Winding Bay Lane
West Palm Beach, FL 33412   USA
peter@peterweisz.com

Menachem Begin Remembered

Hasten, Hart N. • All rights reserved
            Memoir — Biography —Israel — Judaism

ISBN:

Printed in the United States of America Lulu Books.
1 2 3 4 5 6 7 8 9 10

Menachem Begin Remembered

to Simona

Hart N. Hasten

Contents

Introduction 1

Author's Foreword 9

Chapter One: A Man Named Begin.............................11

Chapter Two: Meeting Mr. Begin 17

Chapter Three: A Heritage Shared 23

Chapter Four: I'm a Believer 31

Chapter Five: The Hunter and the Head of State 37

Chapter Six: Blessed Are the Pupils 45

Chapter Seven: A Humble Heart 53

Chapter Eight: The Fourth Estate................................69

Chapter Nine: The Spirit of '76 85

Chapter Ten: Alisa..95

Chapter Eleven: Peacemaker.....................................111

Chapter Twelve: Term Two 135

Chapter Thirteen: Fundraising 145

Chapter Fourteen: A Leader's Legacy.......................161

Photo Album 171

Acknowledgements...193

About the Author..194

Hart N. Hasten

Other Books by Hart Hasten

I Shall Not Die *(2002, Gefen Publishing)*

Hart N. Hasten

Introduction

Hart Hasten is a force of nature as well as a national treasure. I'm proud to say that I have known and admired him for more than fifty years. We had met, in the early 1970s, at a family wedding at which I was officiating. This was during my tenure as the founding Rabbi of the Lincoln Square Synagogue in the newly developed Lincoln Center Cultural area in Manhattan. I recall the way that Hart, even then, spoke enthusiastically to me of Menachem Begin as the next prime minister of Israel. Hart, I soon came to understand, is the living embodiment of the American Dream, and as such, a passionate patriot. But for me he is, along with his beloved wife and life's partner, Simona, first and foremost a devoted Zionist and an avid supporter of the City of Efrat which now comprises nine hilltops in Gush Etzion, an area in Judea that I was privileged to develop, as well as a champion of our educational network, Ohr Torah Stone, including High Schools, Educator's Seminaries and Rabbinical Schools for both men and women.

As I got to know Hart, I learned of his incredible life story. From Holocaust survivor to a respected industry leader, political activist, and major philanthropist, his is an unparalleled saga of struggle and success. If you have not already done so, I urge you to read his inspiring memoir I Shall Not Die. The book's title is drawn from the first portion of a verse from the Book of Psalms (118,8) which is chanted on each of our Jewish Festivals: "I shall not die but I shall live and relate the (wondrous) deeds of G-d." As you will see, this

1

verse characterizes Hart's life as well as my City in Israel, with the important earthly hero in both sagas being Menachem Begin.

One chapter of that book deals with Hart's singular and sustained friendship with former Israeli prime minister, Menachem Begin. Hart has often shared with me his admiration for this man who is today regarded as a revered historic figure and whom Hart considered to be his personal mentor. Hart also would share stories and episodes with me about his relationship with Begin. So, I was particularly gratified to learn that, at age 90, Hart had decided to write this book in which he provides a much closer and more profound personal look at his unique friendship with this singular towering figure of Jewish and world history. I was especially gratified to have been invited to write this Introduction, which will elucidate how Menachem Begin was G-d's emissary who immeasurably enriched both of our lives.

My first salient memory of Menachem Begin is one that I have spoken of and shared with Hart repeatedly. It took place in 1977, shortly after Begin's election to office. His initial trip abroad as Israeli Prime Minister was to the U.S. where his first stop was New York in order to visit several of the world's outstanding Jewish personalities, Rav Soloveitchik, Rav Moshe Feinstein and the Lubavitcher Rebbe. During that period in my life, in addition to my rabbinical position, I was a Talmud teacher (Ram) at Yeshiva University and on the Thursday afternoon of Menachem Begin's scheduled visit with Rav Soloveitchik, I was in a personal meeting with the Rav (as my Rebbe was called by his students) regarding Maimonides theology. Our meeting was interrupted by a phone call which served to inform the Rav that the newly elected prime minister of Israel would be arriving momentarily.

As you will see, this historic and nostalgic reunion between the spiritual and political leaders of world Jewry turned out to be one of the most significant meetings of my life. The Rav had tears coursing out of his eyes as he literally ran to embrace the Prime Minister, with whom he had played as a child during a time that saw him frequently spending Shabbat with his illustrious grandfather, the Brisker Rav. Menachem Begin's father, Binyamin—an avid Zionist and devotee of Revisionist leader, Ze'ev Jabotinsky—was the gabbai (nowadays, he would be considered the president) of the Brisker Rav's synagogue. Both Begin and the Rav began to reminisce. Apparently, the Brisker Rav, they recalled, was the true leader of the synagogue, because only he—and not Binyamin, Menachem Begin's father—held the keys to the Synagogue. And both men agreed that although the gabbai was a strong Zionist and the Brisker Rav was not at all, there was nevertheless great respect between the Rav and the gabbai.

There was only one argument they both remembered. It occurred when Theodor Herzl, the "father" of modern Zionism—but not at all an observant Jew—died in 1904. The gabbai (who was known as a great orator) announced at the end of the early morning service (6:00 A.M.) that he (Binyamin) would deliver a eulogy for Herzl in the synagogue that morning at 10 A.M. The Brisker Rav, who heard the announcement, cried out to the few people who were still in the synagogue: "A non-observant Jew will not be eulogized in my synagogue." The Rav proceeded to take the keys and lock the synagogue door! Needless to say, the Brisker Rav held the only set of keys to the synagogue. When the gabbai returned at 9:30 A.M. and found the synagogue to be sealed shut, he broke open the lock and forced open the doors. With a very warm smile, Menachem Begin said as he ended the story: "We all had the greatest respect for your grandfather, but my father, the Zionist, won that disagreement."

"Yes," agreed the Rav, "and my father told me in the name of my grandfather that at first he was ready to demand the resignation of the gabbai, but first he asked someone who was present for the eulogy how many attendees were there. When he heard that there were 1200 people filling the shul, plus several hundred outside of the synagogue, his position softened. And so, my grandfather told my father: 'A rabbi must know when to cry out and a rabbi must know when to keep silent. If so many people came to a eulogy, it was time for me to be silent.'"

Many years passed by. On the last Sunday night in February 1980, after many long years of planning and lobbying for Efrat, after succeeding in getting government permission to start building our City and after 195 families had given a significant sum of money for a down payment for their homes in Efrat (mostly families from South Africa and America), I arrived at Ben Gurion Airport for what was advertised to have been the laying of the cornerstone for the City of Efrat—only to learn that a Yeshiva student in Hebron, Yehoshua Salome, had been murdered in a terrorist attack. As a result, the Knesset had ordered a moratorium on all new settlements. Moshko (Moshe Moshkowitz), the founder of the entire Gush Etzion Project, met me at the airport to report that I may as well return to New York—at least for the present—since the project of Efrat was dead, at least for the time being. He admitted that we had lost the momentum needed to move ahead.

I refused to give up. In the same way that Theodor Herzl's eulogy had succeeded earlier, hopefully Herzl would have another victory here. Miraculously, a man named Begin was G-d's emissary this time as well. I gathered all of the *protectzia* I could muster and, as a result, Prime Minister Begin agreed to meet me that coming Thursday morning in his Knesset office. I asked my wife and a number of our big financial supporters to fly in for what I prayed might be a momentous meeting. I was not optimistic since only the Prime Minister could undo the Knesset decision; and that only happened rarely.

The prime minister welcomed us most graciously but said that, unfortunately, his hands were tied. The Cabinet had taken a unanimous vote to freeze all new settlement building. I told him how we had been planning Efrat for five years, since 1976, and that 195 families had each given a significant down payment for a home in Efrat. I gave him the list of all the families, many bearing New York addresses. The prime minister had tears in his eyes as he reviewed the list and then turned to look at me very closely.

"You look familiar to me," he said. "Didn't we meet in Rav Soloveitchik's apartment? Did we not speak of how my father broke the lock on the door of the synagogue in Brisk in order to eulogize Theodor Herzl?" I nodded, hardly able to believe that he recognized me from a meeting in which I had not spoken a word! Begin then pronounced: "Let the student of the grandson of the Brisker Rav benefit from the prophecy of Theodor Herzl and build his settlement."

Begin next asked his aide, Yechiel Kadishai, to bring him a copy of Theodor Herzl's classic work, The Jewish State, which was apparently close at hand in the Knesset. After only a few moments of leafing through the pages, Begin read aloud Herzl's vision that, once the Jewish State had become a reality, "Every congregation will settle in the State, each congregation with its rabbi." In an emotion-charged voice, Begin said, "You are fulfilling Herzl's prophecy. How can I stop your progress? I will overrule the decision of the Cabinet. This Sunday you may proceed with the cornerstone-laying ceremony, but with only two government ministers in attendance and without any publicity whatsoever."

I embraced him in gratitude. Somehow, even "with no publicity whatsoever," there were more than 3000 people who attended the event. It was clear that Menachem Begin, and especially G-d, were on the side of Zionism. Coincidence?

In addition to many more such stories about the man Hart calls "my personal hero," in these pages you will discover what, according to Hart, Begin would have thought of such contemporary developments as the Abraham Accords. As a Nobel Peace Prize Laureate for his role in bringing about the Camp David Peace Accords between Israel and Egypt in the 1970s, it was Begin and his legacy that served to inspire those who forged the Abraham Accords that have served to broaden the blessings of peace throughout the region.

It was on the first night of Chanukah in 2020, as the Abraham Accords were being announced to the world, that Hart and I were afforded the honor of lighting the first candle of the giant Chabad Chanukiah at Jerusalem's Mamilla Mall. As I commented to him then: "All of Israel and all of the world must be grateful to Menachem Begin for his legacy that inspired and guided the framers of this historic agreement." As it is written...

> "They shall beat their swords into ploughshares and their spears into pruning hooks: nation shall not lift up sword against nation, neither shall they learn war anymore *(Isaiah 2:4)*."

Zionist, patriot, and activist, it is Hart Hasten's legacy of leadership, represented in part by this book, that will not only allow future generations to revere and remember the formidable historic figure that was Menachem Begin, but will also serve as an enduring testimony to the good works of Hart Hasten himself who, following Begin's example of rectitude, respect, and Jewish pride, has made ours a better nation and made this a better world.

Rabbi Shlomo Riskin

Author's Foreword

Although it seems like only yesterday, as I write these words in 2021, it has been nearly three decades since my hero, mentor, teacher, and friend Menachem Begin passed away. This book is intended as a testament to his memory, marking his thirtieth *yahrzeit*.

In the years since his death, there has been no abatement in the public fascination with Begin's life. I am aware of this phenomenon because, as Begin's friend—both before and after his tenure as Israel's prime minister—I am constantly being asked about the man. It is this enduring interest and admiration that are Begin's legacy and that have led to the creation of this book.

Back in 2002, at the age of seventy, I authored a personal memoir titled *I Shall Not Die*. The book was well received, and the chapter that generated the most positive response was called "Mar Begin." (Mar is a title of respect in Hebrew.) In that chapter, I chronicled my long-standing and unique friendship with Menachem Begin and included a few stories drawn from our years together. Space considerations forced me to limit the number of such episodes, and many memorable moments were omitted. Over the past twenty years, these contact points have not dimmed one bit in my memory. In fact, just the opposite. With each passing year, these precious recollections of encounters with my mentor and friend become ever more precious to me.

Over the years, there have been numerous media events that have stimulated public interest in the life of Menachem Begin. The publication of books such as Yehuda Avner's *The Prime Ministers* in 2010, Avi Shilon's *Menachem Begin: A Life* in 2012, and Daniel Gordis's *Menachem Begin: The Battle for Israel's Soul* in 2014 are three such examples. And in 2020, the release of the outstanding documentary film *Upheaval: The Journey of Menachem Begin* served to heighten interest in and admiration for a leader who is today regarded as a near-biblical figure. It is no surprise, therefore, that Menachem Begin was ranked at the top of the list of most beloved former prime ministers in a survey conducted by the Israeli newspaper *Haaretz*.

In this book, I begin with the information contained in *I Shall Not Die* and then expand upon it. To this I have added glimpses and shared episodes that shine in my memory and will contribute to a more intimate understanding of Begin that may not be gleaned from the sources listed above. It is my hope that I have helped illuminate the soul and spirit of this extraordinary man who humbly described himself as "a simple Jew."

—Hart N. Hasten
December, 2021

Chapter One

A Man Named Begin

I first heard the name Menachem Begin as a teenager in the dis-placed persons (DP) camp where my family was housed immediately after the Holocaust. We had survived the mass destruction of our people as refugees in Kazakhstan, and now, in 1945, we had returned to Europe to try to pick up the pieces and restore our lives. But it was a vastly different world we found. Our idea of seeking to create a Jewish nation moved from dream to necessity. It was in this environ-ment of energized Zionism in which I became a devoted admirer of Menachem Begin.

The political milieu in the DP camps was characterized by layers of complexity and competing crosscurrents. The youth group I had originally joined in Wloclawek, Poland, called Hashomer Hatzair, like the socialist group Dror, was aligned with the leftist ideologies advocating a binational state in Palestine. While this faction represented the majority, I soon switched to Betar, the youth group of Jabotinsky's right-wing Revisionist Party. Betar (an acro-nym for Brit Trumpeldor, named after the Russian martyr who gave his life defending the Land of Israel against Arab attack) believed that Jews needed to reclaim the ancient land from whoever held it, be it Arab or Englishman, in order to establish a modern Jewish state.

It was at this point that I first heard about a man named Begin. His name was whispered with reverence throughout the alleyways and backrooms of all the Jewish DP camps. Menachem Begin was the leader of Etzel—the Irgun Zvai Leumi, the National Military Organization, or simply the Irgun. The Irgun, along with the Haganah, comprised the core of Jewish resistance to the British Mandatory government in Palestine. Jabotinsky was among the founders of the Haganah and headed it till 1920, when he was arrested by the British.

After World War II, both groups—the Irgun and the Haganah—were illegal in Palestine, but since the Haganah, whose Jewish Brigade had served under the British during the war, was viewed as the less extreme of the two, its activities were somewhat tolerated by the authorities. The Irgun, however, was viewed by the British as an underground terrorist organization. During the war, the Haganah had advocated restraint and cooperation in dealing with the British and the Arabs. The Irgun, on the other hand, adopted a more militant posture and vocally called for an immediate revolt against Britain while the war against the Nazis was still being waged.

The Irgun was founded in Palestine by Jabotinsky in 1931 as a non-socialist military arm of the Revisionist Party, whose policies called for the creation of a Jewish state, by force if necessary, on both sides of the Jordan. Despite their calls for liberation from the British, the Irgun had worked secretly with the British against the common Nazi enemy. In fact, one of the Irgun's first leaders—the mysterious military genius David Raziel—was killed while conducting an underground mission to Iraq on behalf of the British Army. The death of the Irgun leader Raziel in 1941, shortly after Jabotinsky's death, took a heavy toll on the Irgun, as did the split led by Avraham Stern. Yaakov Meridor was chosen to head the organization, but soon relinquished command. Meridor was disliked by the Haganah, who eventually turned him over to the British for arrest. Begin, a charismatic Polish/Czech Betar leader who had just recently arrived in Palestine was persuaded to take the reins from Meridor in December 1943. He immediately undertook a tactical campaign of revolt and resistance, which eventually succeeded in driving the British out of Palestine.

During the critical years of 1946 and 1947, the British had placed a price on Begin's head, and this fact only made him more of a hero to our Betar group. Begin and the Irgun were soundly whipping the British in Palestine. Stories of his activities filled us with an entirely new emotion: Jewish pride, or what Jabotinsky referred to as "hadar." While I was brought up by my father and grandfather with a strong sense of pride in the history of the Jewish people, this was different. My newfound pride arose from what my fellow Jews were doing in Palestine right now ... not two thousand years ago.

Begin's voice was an inspiring call to arms to all the displaced and dispossessed young Jews of Europe. "You are the Hebrew soldiers," he would declare. He would often repeat Jabotinsky's well-known admonition: "The blood of the Maccabees flows in your veins!" Begin's words held a resonance that went beyond mere youthful romanticism. There was a flavor to his rhetoric that transcended our recent history and tapped into the most basic ancient roots of the Jewish people.

On February 1, 1944, Begin's well-known "Proclamation of the Revolt" was first distributed by leaflet throughout Palestine, after having been broadcast over the Irgun's clandestine radio station. Betar groups like ours circulated the proclamation throughout the DP camps. With my glue bucket and "Rak Kach" (the Irgun motto: "Only thus") posters, I became known as a prolific pamphleteer. I would often show up in class with hundreds of such leaflets stuffed under my shirt. An excerpt from the proclamation:

Hebrews!

The establishment of the Hebrew Government and the realization of its program is the sole way to rescue our people, to save our existence and our honor. We will go in this path, because there is no other. We will fight. Every Jew in the state will fight.

Hebrews!

The fighting youth will not be deterred by victims, blood, and suffering. It will not surrender, it will not rest, as long as our days have not been renewed as of old, as long as our people is not assured of a state, freedom, honor, bread, righteousness, and justice. And if you will surely aid it, then your eyes will soon see in our time the return to Zion and the renaissance of Israel. This and more may G-d grant us!

—Excerpt from the Proclamation of the Revolt, 1944

The Insignia of the Irgun Zvai Leumi

We shared a certain bravado and toughness born from not only recent experiences but also an unnatural selection process. We were the only Jews from our town who had the wherewithal to pack up and flee the advancing Nazis. Those who did not share this tenacity were gone. Similarly, while survival during the Holocaust was mostly a matter of luck, to survive also required toughness and resilience. Most young people in the camps shared these qualities, for those who did not—those who had complacently failed to recognize the impending Nazi onslaught—had mostly been lost in the crucible of the Holocaust. We admired these qualities in Begin and in his philosophy. He was my hero, and I was prepared and eager to follow his leadership.

This admiration was shared by my older brother, Mark *(z"l)* who, like me, underwent training by the Irgun, and who eventually sailed to Israel aboard the ill-fated *Altalena*. Our dedication at this time was so great that we were prepared to lay down our lives in behalf of the noble cause championed by Menachem Begin.

Another factor that contributed to our toughness was that the Betar leadership was training us teenagers in weapons combat. Carrying a pistol, I regularly engaged in target practice and small arms drills in the forests near the camp. We knew we were being molded into Irgun soldiers, trained to fight the British, the Arabs, and anyone else that stood in the way of a Jewish nation in Palestine.

While our family never fit the stereotype of the eternally victimized *shtetl* Jew—we had too much Jewish pride for that—I felt that Begin and Betar represented a metamorphosis. A tough new Jew was emerging from the ashes—one filled with pride and a love of Zion, ready to fight to reclaim and defend our nation, not bound by the tired, failed ideologies of socialism, and no longer willing to suffer the blows and insults of the bigot and antisemite. This was the Jew of the future. Thanks to Menachem Begin, this was the Jew I became in the DP camps, and the Jew I remain to this day.

Chapter Two

Meeting Mr. Begin

My parents and I immigrated to the US in 1951 when I was nine-teen years old. Thanks to the opportunities to be found only in America, I was, by the late 1960s, in the process of building a successful business and a wonderful Jewish family. But, throughout those years, I never abandoned my admiration for my hero, Menachem Begin. I observed for years the honorable manner in which he led the loyal opposition in Israeli politics. When I had reached the point where I was able to substantially support the State of Israel, it afforded me the opportunity to finally meet my hero face-to-face.

One of the first Jewish causes with which I became involved—as soon as I was in a position to do so—was Israel Bonds. The Israel Bond movement was started in 1951 by David Ben-Gurion, among others, as a means of raising revenues badly needed by the young Israeli government. The idea was to build a "bond" between Israel and its supporters around the world through the creation of a financial instrument. Investors, in addition to earning a market rate of return, would have a stake in the future of Israel. If enough bondholders could be created, the effort would yield far-reaching political, as well as economic, objectives. Money raised through the sale of Israel Bonds is typically used to finance the many nonmilitary projects carried out by the Israeli government, such as highways, bridges, canals, power plants and the like. But unlike other types of foreign securities, Israel Bonds are not sold through broker-age houses. Instead they are marketed using a fund-raising model. Bond dinners, where investors are encouraged to stand up and publicly announce their purchase of Israel Bonds, are commonplace. Israel Bonds offices operate in major cities across America handling transactions and working with lay volunteers to organize bond drives. It was in my capacity as an Israel Bonds leader that I was afforded the opportunity to meet, in person, the man who had been my life-long hero, Menachem Begin.

Since Israeli independence in 1948, Begin had served as the leader of the largest non-Labor political party in Israel. As discussed earlier, Begin's Irgun Zvai Leumi Jewish underground was a key factor in the establishment of the State of Israel. During the revolt against the British Mandate, Begin had ordered the Akko (Acre) prison breakout and the destruction of the central British administrative offices at the King David Hotel.

After Israeli independence, Begin, as leader of the Herut Party, served as head of the loyal opposition during the long tenure of the prevailing Ben-Gurion Mapai Party. It was in this capacity that he led the movement against the acceptance of German reparations for the Nazi Holocaust. In 1965 Begin merged the Herut Party with the Liberals to form Gahal, which would later serve as the foundation for the Likud Party. The crisis atmosphere of 1967 saw the creation of a national unity government that brought Begin to the cabinet table. It was in this role that he visited Chicago in 1969 as the keynote speaker on behalf of Israel Bonds.

When I got word that Begin would be speaking at the Chicago bond dinner, I immediately made plans to attend. I was hoping to listen to the hero of my youth and perhaps shake his hand. As I moved through the reception line at the black-tie soirée, I introduced myself and offered a few words in Yiddish:

"I've waited all my life to shake your hand, Mar Begin. You were a hero to all of us in Betar when we were stuck in the DP camps," I said eagerly.

"You? You were in Betar?" He looked a bit confused. Finding an "Etzelnik" here among these American fat cats appeared to catch him off guard. "Where are you from? Where were you during the war?"

"I'm from Galicia, and we survived the war in Kazakhstan." I didn't want to hold up the line, so I answered hurriedly and made to move on. "Wait! Let's have a word afterwards," he called as I nodded gladly.

Begin's remarks that night were stirring and succeeded in motivating the assemblage to new heights of Israel Bonds investment. Sometimes when a person meets a hero in the flesh, there is a sense of disappointment as the legend becomes humanized. There was none of that with Begin. I was enthralled with his powerful message. He spoke in English with heartfelt passion about the recent unification of Jerusalem and its impact on the future of Israel. He was still something of a firebrand, but his current role as cabinet minister had seemed to mellow his rhetoric a bit. True to his word, he graciously approached our table afterwards and engaged me in an extraordinary chat.

Begin was curious about my family, and when I told him that my brother was aboard the *Altalena*, he seemed very pleased. I shared stories about how we distributed his words in the camps and how they provided hope and pride to our shattered numbers. I recounted my personal history to Begin, and he was quite moved. I recall a couple of Israeli VIPs coming over to our table to greet Begin, who immediately introduced me and said:

"You must meet my friend, Mr. Hasten. Do you know what this kid went through during the Shoah? He had next to no chance of survival, and yet he made it!" Over the years Begin would retell my story repeatedly whenever he introduced me to someone new. I was amazed at how he always got the details exactly right, and I became convinced that he enjoyed a truly photographic memory.

The genuine warmth I felt from this man reminded me so very much of my own father. The friendship we developed over the next twenty-five years, I can proudly say, was every bit a "father and son" relationship. We developed an immediate and lasting linkage that night in Chicago, and as the conversation wound down, Begin pressed my arm and leaned closer: "You must look me up the next time you're in Israel." He gave me his home address and phone number and bade me good night.

Although I had not mentioned it to Begin, at this point, I had yet to set foot on Israeli soil. I made up my mind that night, however, that I would travel there as soon as possible. I signed up for the next UJA (United Jewish Appeal) mission to Israel in January of 1970.

Of course, being in Israel for the first time was a transcendent experience. It felt strangely dreamlike and yet spiritually charged with the electricity generated by thousands of years of Jewish yearning. It was a homecoming to be sure, and yet I was too excited to feel at home. The sight of thousands of Jews, strolling down boulevards, emerging from Jewish shops—simply living normal everyday lives—caused my heart to overflow.

The moment that has stayed with me, as I'm sure it has for many Jews, was my first glimpse of the Kotel, the Western Wall, in Jerusalem. I rushed there as soon as I entered the city, and my emotions overcame me as I observed the ancient edifice. Gazing through my tears, I was permeated with a strange feeling of having somehow been here before. It wasn't simply a déjà vu, but rather a sense of wholeness or completion in the pit of my psyche. After over a hundred journeys to Jerusalem in the past fifty years, a visit to the Kotel is still my first stop.

I phoned Begin as soon as I arrived at my hotel in Jerusalem, and he suggested we meet for breakfast. When I asked where, his answer gave me pause. He suggested we meet at the King David Hotel. Begin, of course, had been wanted by the British when, as head of the Irgun, he had ordered the bombing of this hotel, which housed the British administrative offices.

"Don't you feel odd coming here?" I inquired after we had taken our seats.

"Actually, I like to come here ... but not for the reason you think," he replied with a hint of a smile. "When I first arrived in Palestine as a private in the Polish Army, I attempted to come in the front door of this hotel. I was stopped by a Polish officer, who informed me that enlisted men could not enter this way and that I was obliged to employ the back door. The front door was only for officers. I kept trying, but I was always stopped. I think about that every time I visit here and enter through the front door with no problem." He made no further reference to the bombing and I left it at that.

Begin was absolutely fascinated with my story. He probed me and devoured every detail. As we spoke, I could sense a kinship being forged. This man had been my hero since my youth, and now here I was, relating stories from that period to him face-to-face. "We admired you because you fought back," I explained. I believe he could also sense that I had attempted to pattern my life to encompass many of the same traits I had observed in him. Tenacity, courage, direct action. These were values I learned from my father and observed in Begin years ago. But our discussions also centered on the here and now. As leader of the minority Herut Party, Begin was in constant need of support, both political and financial. I sensed that Begin viewed me as someone who could be groomed for leadership in advancing his current political agenda in the US. It was these forces that formed the foundation of our lasting friendship.

Chapter Three

A Heritage Shared

*As I got to know Menachem Begin, we quickly discovered numer-
ous similarities in our backgrounds. In this chapter, I discuss a few of
them.*

Many who know of my friendship with Menachem Begin
have asked me the following sly question: "I understand
what attracted you to this great man, but what attracted
Begin to you?" The question is usually accompanied by a friendly
smile. Actually, it's a matter that I have also wondered about and to
which I have devoted some thought. The answer is that we shared
many significant interconnections. Here is a brief list:

- We both emerged from the heart of Poland.
- Our mother tongue in both cases was Yiddish.
- We were both blessed with clear-thinking fathers who were re-
  alists.
- As teenagers, we were both members of Hashomer Hatzair.
- We both lived for years in the Soviet Union and learned to
  speak Russian.
- Like Begin, I consider myself an observant Jew with a high
  reverence for Jewish tradition.
- Tragically, we both witnessed our close family members perish
  at the hands of the Nazis.

The most significant similarity arose from our family backgrounds. Like Begin's father, Ze'ev Dov, my father, Dov, was a passionate Zionist. They were both men who believed in seeing things the way they really are. We were both taught by our fathers that communism represented a worthless ideology and were both introduced to the thinking of Theodore Herzl and the passion of Ze'ev Jabotinsky. Although we were brought up in different regions—Begin in Brest-Litovsk in what is today Belarus, while I was born in the Galitzia region of Poland, today the Ukraine—both areas were located at the intersection of Eastern and Central Europe, and hence our cultural influences likewise overlapped.

Begin was eighteen years my senior, yet there were also many overlaps in our formative years. The first that comes to mind was our use of language. As boys we both spoke Yiddish and Polish at home, and Hebrew at *cheder* (school). Once we met, we discovered that we had both learned to speak Russian, he while imprisoned in Siberia and I when our family languished in Kazakhstan during the war. Of course by that time we both spoke fluent English, and this was the language we chose to speak between us.

Another point of intersection that may surprise those aware of our common right-wing political leanings is the fact that, as teenagers, we both were members of the socialist Zionist scouting movement known as Hashomer Hatzair (the Young Guard). Founded in Galicia in 1913, the group is the oldest Zionist youth movement still in existence today. Initially adhering to Marxist-Zionist ideology, the group believed that the liberation of Jewish youth could be accomplished by "aliyah," or immigration to Palestine. The movement grew rapidly after World War I, reaching Lithuania and Belarus, where Begin was introduced to it.

I am sure that Begin's reasons for joining Hashomer were identical to my own. It was simply the only option available in those days for a young Jew to express his solidarity with those building a Zionist homeland in Palestine. But as we matured, the socialist ideology of Hashomer lost its appeal. We were both about the same age when we came to understand that the world would not hand the Jews a homeland on a silver platter, and if we wanted one, we had to get tough and learn to fight for it. It was at this point in our lives that we both joined Betar, the youth wing of Jabotinsky's Revisionist Party. By the time I joined Betar, after the war, Begin had risen to become its dynamic leader.

Like me, Menachem Begin made no apologies for the leftist leanings of his youth. Although he was no great admirer of Winston Churchill, he nevertheless appreciated this quote that was attributed to him: "If you're not a liberal when you're 21, you have no heart. If you're not a conservative by the time you're 35, you have no brain."

In his later years, Begin came to appreciate and even admire Churchill. During his years of seclusion, I would often bring Begin books from America—books of the type I knew he preferred reading: histories and biographies. He was a voracious reader, often digesting a book cover-to-cover in a single day. I recall how excited and animated he became when I brought him the three-volume set of *Churchill & Roosevelt; the Complete Correspondence* (Princeton University Press, 1987). At my next visit, he told me he had plowed through the entire collection nonstop in five days. He then admitted:

"I had always thought that FDR was the greater leader. But now, I see that it was really Churchill." Although both men, he noted, could have done much more to save Jewish lives from the Nazis.

The most profound formative experience that Begin and I shared was the indelible impact of the Holocaust. Begin spoke often of how the lessons of that tragic time of darkness had shaped his thinking and accounted for his persona as a proud and strong Jew who understood the true cost of weakness. In fact, Begin was frequently accused by his political rivals of being "obsessed with the Holocaust." Although pundits in the media would suggest that he put those negative memories behind him and focus on the bright future, Begin never forfeited his focus on the Holocaust. How could he? His beloved family had been consumed by it.

Begin's father was among the 500 Brest-Litovsk Jews rounded up by the Nazis at the end of June 1941 and brutally shot or drowned in the Bug River. Both his beloved mother, Hassia, and his older brother, Hertz, had likewise perished in the flames.

As Prime Minister, Begin invoked these memories often as in the following excerpt from remarks delivered in the Knesset on Yom HaShoah (Holocaust Remembrance Day) in 1981:

> The Germans pushed them into the River Bug. They opened fire with machine guns from both sides, and the river became red with blood. The water turned to blood. That is how they died. And my mother—she was an old woman, sick in hospital. They summoned her and all the sick women in the hospital, and slaughtered them. So, yes, I don't deny it—I live with this. It colors everything I do. I will live with this until the day I die.

Sadly, I too am haunted by similar memories. On the day the Germans arrived to our town, my 70-year-old beloved *zayde* (grandfather), a man I worshiped and adored, was among the Jews ordered to assemble in the town's square by the bloodthirsty and barbaric *Einsatzgruppen.* As a respected elder of the town's Jewish community, my *zayde* was ordered by the commandant to step forward. He did so holding the hand of my first cousin, his 10-year-old grandson, Lonka, who was exactly my age and my best friend in the world. When my *zayde* was commanded to serve as the head the *Judenrat,* the council that would coordinate with the Nazis in the deportation of the town's Jews, he bravely and defiantly refused. The commandant methodically removed his pistol and, before my cousin's horrified eyes and before the entire community, proceeded to shoot my *zayde* in the head. When my little cousin, Lonka, screamed in shock, he was afforded the same merciless fate. Thus they became the first victims of the mass slaughter that was soon to follow.

With the exception of my parents and older brother, all my other family members were systematically murdered shortly thereafter. This shared sense of unfathomable loss was a factor that bound Begin and me together in a way that I cannot fully describe in words. It may be best understood as a mostly unspoken reaction to the unspeakable. We have both looked into what Elie Wiesel described as "the void that remains when man abandons all morality." One can never be the same after that.

In later life, when Begin was asked by a reporter to list the lessons that may be drawn from the Holocaust, he provided six points, with this one leading the list:

> First, if an enemy of our people says he seeks to destroy us, believe him. Don't doubt him for a moment. Don't make light of it. Do all in your power to deny him the means of carrying out his satanic intent.

My father in fact did not doubt that the Germans meant it when they said they would destroy us. And it was this fact that saved the four of us—my parents, my brother, and me—from the cruel fate that befell every other member of our family. Unlike so many others facing the Nazi onslaught, my father confronted the reality of our situation honestly. He was, above all, a realist who did not allow himself to indulge in the temporary comfort of denial. My father was convinced that Hitler wasn't kidding when he promised to eliminate all the Jews and he was willing to accept the evidence of that promise when he encountered it. When Jews fleeing eastward passed through our town with tales of unbelievable atrocities, my father listened to them and believed them. Thus, thanks to his blessed foresight, my father packed us up on a horse-drawn wagon and led us eastward towards eventual safety, fleeing just days before the Germans killing squads arrived.

I have always felt that an angel whispered the following words into my father's ear:

Lech lecha me'artzecha umimoladetecha umibeit avicha (Get yourself out of this land, from your birthplace, and from your father's house). According to the book of Genesis, these are the words spoken by G-d to Abram directing him to leave his home and travel to "the land I will show you."

In a parallel manner, Begin's father was influenced by the words of Revisionist leader Ze'ev Jabotinsky, who came to Brest-Litovsk in the 1920s and exhorted the town's Jews with his stirring oratory and his prescient pronouncements.

First, the struggle for the creation of a Jewish state must, by necessity, be a military one, he said. Neither the British, installed as Mandatory overseers of Palestine, nor the indigenous Arabs would willingly turn over any land without being forced to do so militarily. Second, having a firsthand familiarity with the shortcomings of the Bolshevik system, he warned against the naïve notion of establishing a socialist Jewish state. And, most prophetically, Jabotinsky called upon the Jews of Eastern Europe to evacuate before it was too late. "Liquidate the diaspora," he admonished them, "or else it will liquidate you."

By the time the Germans conquered Brest-Litovsk on June 22, 1941, Begin's father was nearly sixty. Although he believed in the truth of Jabotinsky's warning and taught his son to believe it, at that point he did not have the means nor the opportunity to act upon those beliefs.

These are but a few of the common threads in the fabric of our respective family backgrounds that serve as the foundation of our friendship. It was upon this foundation that my respect and admiration for Menachem Begin was built over the years as I observed him become the premier Jewish leader of our generation. It is for this reason that I still look to him as my role model to this day.

Chapter Four

I'm A Believer

By the early 1970s I was deeply involved as president of the new Jewish day school we had founded in Indianapolis. Obtaining funding from the local Jewish community, however, was a distinct challenge. Our community's major philanthropic agency, the Jewish Federation, operated under the misguided control of liberal lay and professional leaders who viewed my support of Menachem Begin as a right-wing pipe dream. Despite this disdain, I never lost my conviction that Begin would someday succeed in his quest to become Israel's prime minister.

Over the next few years I would meet with Begin whenever I traveled to Israel. We would also get together during his visits to the US. In 1973 I succeeded in bringing him to Indianapolis for an Israel Bonds dinner and showed him around our fledgling day school. He was deeply moved by the experience, sharing details of his visit with his wife Alisa upon his return. After this visit, both Begin and Alisa would always inquire about the school whenever we would meet. I recall a discussion with Jewish Federation director Frank Newman shortly before the event:

"Who are you bringing in as a speaker for this year's bond dinner, Hart?" he asked me.

"I've invited Menachem Begin, the leader of the opposition party in Israel, to speak," I replied.

"Oh, then you shouldn't expect a very big turnout," he commented disdainfully.

"Why's that?" I asked.

"Well, everyone knows that Begin's a fascist."

This comment shocked and stunned me. "Where did he get that from?" I wondered. Begin was no fascist. He was a true Zionist patriot. "He must have been listening to Ben-Gurion," I concluded, since Ben-Gurion's animosity and jealousy of Begin were well known.

Despite Newman's warning, we sold a record number of tickets to the dinner, although there was one fellow who did not buy one. The chairman of the Jewish Federation's executive committee and my nemesis in our battle over support for the Hebrew Academy did not wish to be seen attending an event featuring such a right-wing "fanatic" as Begin. Nevertheless, he was very interested in personally hearing what the man had to say. I recall catching a glimpse of this fellow, who had snuck in after everyone was seated and was now standing in the corridor outside the ballroom, listening intently throughout Begin's speech.

At this time, my brother Mark and I had agreed to serve as Israel Bond co-chairs for our community. This role had secured me a seat on the national executive committee working under the leadership of Sam Rothberg, one of the founders of Israel Bonds. In this capacity I was involved in putting together bond missions to Israel. Bondholders and potential bondholders were encouraged to visit Israel in order to witness how their investment dollars were being deployed and also for them to draw inspiration intended to stimulate further purchases.

These groups would be addressed by a running stream of Israeli dignitaries. Invariably I would note that the agendas only included "Ma-
painiks," or members of Ben-Gurion's party. I would frequently
complain about this practice and always succeeded in getting a few
Herut leaders, sometimes Begin himself, on the mission agenda. In
this way, a more balanced and accurate picture of Israel's political
diversity was presented to the visitors.

Initially, in response to my pressure, the Herut speaker would be
given a spot on Friday night's agenda. Such events were very poorly
attended since most participants made private plans for the Sabbath.
Also, because of the Sabbath sanctions, no microphone amplification
was permitted and speechmaking was severely impaired. After a few
such debacles, I learned my lesson. As the agendas were being for-
mulated I would insist: "I want Menachem Begin to speak to the
group ... and NOT on Friday night!" I even, at times, had to threaten
to boycott the mission if my wishes were not carried out. I didn't like
using such strong-arm tactics, but I was fervent in my belief that Begin should get his story out to as large an audience as possible. Particularly to affluent Americans who were in a position to offer financial support.

At this stage, Begin had been leading the political opposition to
the prevailing Mapai Party for roughly twenty-five years. He was
labeled in the media as a "former Irgun terrorist" and was falsely described as intransigent, radical, truculent, and worse. The common
wisdom was that both Begin and his Herut Party would forever be a
voice in the wilderness, never destined for Israeli political leadership.
I, however, felt differently. I could see in Begin an intellectual capac-

ity and firmness of character lacking among the members of Israel's ruling party. I came to believe that Begin could be, should be, and would be the next prime minister of Israel, and it was in the following manner that I would introduce him to audiences both in the US and in Israel.

"Ladies and gentlemen, it gives me great pleasure to introduce to you the next prime minister of the State of Israel, the honorable Menachem Begin." Israel's changing demographics along with internal Israeli political dynamics would soon prove me correct.

In Begin I observed an almost Trumanesque rectitude and earthy collegiality that was such a departure from the seamy Mapai/Labor political hacks. Over the years, I had occasion to meet and to know twelve of Israel's fourteen prime ministers (I never met Moshe Sharett or Levi Eshkol). The animosity exhibited by the Labor leadership toward anything religious, and particularly toward the religious right, was pronounced. "How could the future of the Jewish people be entrusted to those who held our heritage in such low esteem?" I wondered. Begin was different. He was fanatically faithful to his wife, Alisa, and while certainly no ascetic, I never observed him in an undignified posture. Furthermore, he was a traditional and educated Jew whose political underpinnings all emanated from the Torah.

After his election as prime minister in 1977, Begin would frequently make mention of my early support. "You believed I would become prime minister before I believed it myself," he would often say, and he was right. I wasn't merely blowing smoke when I introduced him in that way. I sincerely believed that he was the right man for the job. I had the chance to observe all of the players on Israel's political landscape and I came away convinced that Begin's qualifications were the most impressive. If only he could somehow overcome all the old Irgun/Herut baggage that the press continued to burden him with. From the earliest days of statehood, when Ben-Gurion would not even dare to utter Begin's name in public, preferring instead to refer to him as "the leader of the opposition" or "that man sitting next to Dr. Bader," Begin had borne the stigma of the extremist element. But I knew the man, and hence I could see him as he really was: a deeply compassionate Israeli patriot with absolutely no interest in self-aggrandizement.

"This is the manner of man who should lead the Jewish state," I would often think to myself during those years. A man who recognizes that we are the inheritors of an ancient civilization that profoundly shaped the ethical and religious makeup of Western civilization. And then, in a miraculous moment in 1977, the "man who should be prime minister" became the "man who would be prime minister."

Hart N. Hasten

Chapter Five

The Hunter and the Head of State

Once Menachem Begin had been elected prime minister of Israel, people quickly began to regard me as a person with access to a world leader. Naturally, I had to be very judicious about exercising that entrée and not exploiting the special relationship I enjoyed. However, when a request came my way to schedule a meeting between Prime Minister Begin and Simon Wiesenthal, I responded and wasted no time in making the arrangements.

Simon Wiesenthal was a famed Nazi hunter whom I had first gotten to know in the Ebelsberg DP camp in Austria, where my family spent several years after World War II. He, like me, was born in Galicia in what is today the Ukraine. Wiesenthal's birthplace, Buczacz, is located some 50 miles southeast of our family's hometown of Bohorodchany. Wiesenthal was working as an architect in Lvov when the war broke out. He survived the horrors of extermination camps and death marches, winding up at Mauthausen, where he was liberated by the Allies.

I recall Wiesenthal visiting our apartment at Ebelsberg and chatting with my father, a fellow *Galitziano* who always referred to him as "Engineer Wiesenthal." The title was important because such things helped us to overcome the dehumanization that the Nazis had put us through.

After emerging from the DP camps, Wiesenthal had settled in Vienna, where he dedicated his life to tracking down fugitive Nazi war criminals. In 1961 he opened the Documentation Centre of the Association of Jewish Victims of the Nazi Regime. It is said that his efforts played a role in the capture and trial of Adolf Eichmann. He also was instrumental in capturing the commandant of the Sobibor and Treblinka extermination camps, Franz Stangl. Wiesenthal became well known when he exposed the Nazi connections of UN Secretary-General Kurt Waldheim. A fictionalized version of Wiesenthal appeared as the hero of the novel by Ira Levin titled *The Boys from Brazil*. In the 1978 film adaptation, his character was portrayed by Laurence Olivier. Ben Kingsley portrayed the actual Wiesenthal in the 1989 HBO film *Murderers Among Us: The Simon Wiesenthal Story,* as did Judd Hirsch in the Amazon Prime series called *Hunters* in 2020.

In 1977, I again met Simon Wiesenthal as he and Rabbi Marvin Hier enlisted my support for what was to become the Simon Wiesenthal Center in Los Angeles. Five years later I was contacted by Rabbi Hier, now the center's director, who asked if I could arrange a meeting between Wiesenthal, who was then 72, and the prime minister. I agreed to try and contacted Yechiel Kadishai, the director of the Prime Minister's Office.

The arrangements were made for a meeting at a time when Wiesenthal and I would both be in Jerusalem a few months hence. I was typically in the habit of arranging for the prime minister to meet with individuals at his office. But this was different. Begin suggested that we hold the meeting at his home where the atmosphere was less formal. It was simply an opportunity for two men of international stature, who admired each other greatly, to meet one another in person. I was assured that Wiesenthal wanted nothing more from the prime minister than the opportunity to shake his hand and chat. And that is exactly what took place.

After the introductions were made by me and Rabbi Hier, the two men sat down and I became a fly on the wall. What I found interesting at first was the distinctly different dialects of Yiddish employed by the two men. Wiesenthal's Yiddish was the *Galitzianer* variety while Begin's was markedly *Litvish*, as spoken in northeastern Europe. You might compare it to a conversation between a native of Brooklyn and one from Little Rock. They understood each other clearly, but if I closed my eyes, it was easy to tell which man was doing the talking.

The distinction, however, extended beyond language. Just as a Brooklyn stereotypical personality type is different from that of someone from the Deep South, so it was with the varieties of Jewish cultures that populated Eastern Europe before the war. Begin's demeanor, like his speech, was more formal and structured, while Wiesenthal was the more fiery and overtly impassioned.

During my five and a half years spent in the DP camps, I came across Jews from every Eastern and Central European community, from Ukranians to Bessarabians. I found it fascinating to observe the different ways that people from different regions adjusted differently to life in the DP camp. I found the Jews from Czechoslovakia to be the most well adjusted and thereby the friendliest and nicest to deal with. I can honestly say that I never met a Jewish Czech I didn't like.

The non-observant Hungarian Jews from Budapest, on the other hand, had a rough time. This was due, I concluded, to the fact that they had been the most highly assimilated among the Jews of Eastern Europe. The more a Jew felt that he had been part of the mainstream dominant culture, the more outrage he felt at being singled out and oppressed as a Jew.

As I sat quietly and listened to the conversations between two men whom I considered to be archetypes of Eastern European Jewish culture, I noted how they discussed the Shoah, the current political situation and then moved on to an issue that harkened back to a battle waged some thirty years earlier. The issue of German reparations (or as they say in German: *wiedergutmachen*, which literally means "to make things good again" as if the payment of money could somehow transform pure evil into goodness) was a topic that both men felt strongly about. This was not surprising given the highly developed sense of justice that they shared. The question of reparations had been, in the early days of the state, a divisive issue. It was due to Begin's vehement opposition to reparations that he was falsely branded by David Ben-Gurion as a "demagogue."

Begin vociferously maintained that Israel accepting money from Germany in consideration of its crimes against the Jewish people was tantamount to granting them a pardon. In January 1952, Begin addressed a rally of some 15,000 supporters in Jerusalem in which he passionately proclaimed: "Jews cannot accept blood money from our murderers." He spoke directly to Ben-Gurion in reference to the *Altalena* episode, during which Ben-Gurion had ordered the firing of what he labeled "the holy cannon" against the ship that bore Begin and his Irgun followers and that had gone aground in Tel Aviv harbor:

"When you fired at me with that cannon, I gave the order 'Don't. Don't return fire. Exercise restraint.' But today I will give the order 'Do!' This is not the time for restraint." The crowd marched toward the Knesset on King George Street and began throwing stones at the building and the police. Hundreds were injured and arrested. The government-dominated press condemned Begin as a provocateur, and despite the protestations, on September 10, 1952, the reparations agreement between West Germany and Israel was signed in Luxembourg by Chancellor Konrad Adenauer and Israeli Foreign Minister Moshe Sharett. The terms called for Germany to pay Israel close to three billion Deutschmarks (about 3/4 of a billion or $7.5 billion in today's dollars) over the ensuing 12 years.

Begin's opposition was based not only on his moral disgust at placing a price tag on Jewish lives: "Future generations will look back on us and see that we sat around a table with our enemies and negotiated a price for the extermination of our people," he warned. He was also prescient in his understanding about the precedent that such reparations represented.

"Our enemies will question why only the Jews took this money. Why not the Serbs? Or the Greeks? Or the other peoples who were harmed by the Nazis? And our acceptance of it will only fuel their hatred of us and cause them to accuse us of collaboration and manipulation," he said at the time.

Begin's unheeded warnings proved to be prophetic. In June 2019 a spot appeared repeatedly on Al Jazeera television in which a so-called "history teacher" presented this twisted and perverted lesson:

"During World War II, an agreement was reached between Nazi Germany and the Jewish Agency. The acceptance of German reparations by Israel after the war is evidence of Israeli complicity with the Nazis. The fact that only Jews were given such money is proof that the Holocaust actually benefitted the Jews of the world." This vile piece of antisemitic propaganda was viewed by millions of people on YouTube before being removed by Al Jazeera.

During the 1982 meeting I witnessed between Begin and Wiesenthal, the famed Nazi hunter expressed his full support of Begin's thirty-year-old opposition to German reparations. Wiesenthal understood that Begin's opposition, like his own, was based on something more than intellectual consideration. It arose from the personal tragedies the men had endured at the loss of their beloved family members. Begin expressed this personal dimension eloquently when rose in opposition to Israel's acceptance of German reparation and addressed the Knesset as follows:}

In 1919 a tragedy took place in Pinsk, a city near my hometown of Brest-Litovsk. An antisemitic Polish general gathered thirty-four Jews, whom he suspected of being Bolsheviks, lined them up against a brick wall, and executed them by firing squad. When I was a child we were taught to recite a poem memorializing that tragedy. This was at a time before Jewish slaughter was measured in the millions, and the murder of thirty-four Jews was still considered shocking. An international investigation was launched and the American ambassador to Turkey and the father of the future US Treasury Secretary, Henry Morgenthau Sr., was dispatched to Pinsk. He argued that the Polish government should offer monetary compensation to the grieving families. Even though they denied responsibility, the Polish government agreed to make the payments. The Zionist executive committee of Pinsk objected to the payments and said to the families:

"If you accept this money, you will betray the memory of the martyrs and you will be disgraced forever. It will be said that the Jews sold the souls of their loved ones for money. Only if the murderers will be punished, then their sins may be pardoned."

The money was refused by all of the victims' families. How is it then, that the Jews of Pinsk comprehended what was at stake in 1919 while the government of Israel, in 1951, could not?

Wiesenthal commiserated and lamented the fact that Israel's early leadership made many serious mistakes. He pointed out that it was Begin's level-headed restraint that had averted a civil war after the *Altalena* episode and again at the time that German reparations were accepted by Israel. Although I sat in silence, I wished I could likewise chime in to express my admiration for Begin's courageous and ethical leadership.

Afterwards, both Rabbi Hier and Simon Wiesenthal thanked me for setting up the meeting and expressed how much it had meant to them. It had meant a great deal to me as well.

Chapter Six

Blessed Are the Pupils

Ironically, one of the most important lessons that a leader can teach you is how to be a follower. The bonds that linked me with Menachem Begin as my mentor were fashioned after observing the manner in which he exhibited his respect toward his own hero, Ze'ev Jabotinsky.

Over the years I have been most fortunate to receive a number of awards and honors in recognition of my volunteer activities. I'm not certain if I was always deserving, but I do know that I'm appreciative of each such distinction. One such award that I am most proud of is named after Menachem Begin's mentor, Revisionist leader Ze'ev Jabotinsky. The Jabotinsky Medal was presented in October of 1980 to one hundred distinguished Americans—among whom I was included—by the Herut Zionists of America in order to mark the centennial of Ze'ev Jabotinsky's birth.

I recall attending the awards ceremony in New York along with the other 99 recipients. Since we were seated in alphabetical order, I found myself next to the well-known televangelist, Jerry Falwell. Falwell was an Evangelical Christian and staunch Zionist who had likewise been named as a recipient. Prime Minister Menachem Begin flew in to New York to celebrate the Jabotinsky centennial and was on hand to present the medals.

It was a stunning event that saw each guest receive—in addition to the medal—a keepsake souvenir journal featuring a portrait of Jabotinsky on the cover. The painting had been commissioned especially for this event and 350 prints, signed and numbered by the artist, Avi Schwartz, had been distributed to the guests. I recall seeing one of the prints years later in 2015, framed and hanging in the office of Israeli President Reuven Rivlin. I felt pride in the fact that, while the president's print was number 49 of 350, the one hanging in my office was number 1.

I had likewise felt pride at the event when, after shaking hands with all of the prior recipients, including Falwell, when Begin came to me, he not only placed the medal around my neck but he also singled me out by embracing me in a warm public hug.

During the very moving awards ceremony, the story was once again told of Jabotinsky's legacy. He had died suddenly in 1940 while visiting a Betar summer camp in New York and was buried in New York City. His widow announced at the time that Jabotinsky had left instructions that it was his desire for the head of state of the new Zionist nation to order his remains moved there once such a state had been established. It would be eight years before the State of Israel was born under the leadership of David Ben-Gurion. But, so strong was Ben-Gurion's revulsion toward the Revisionist movement that he could not bring himself to issue the order to bring Jabotinsky's remains to Israel. It was left up to a subsequent prime minister, Levi Eshkol, to issue the directive for Jabotinsky's reburial at Mount Herzl in early 1964. I recall how Menachem Begin served as one of Jabotinsky's pallbearers at the time.

Shortly after attending the Jabotinsky Medal awards ceremony in New York, Begin traveled home to Jerusalem, whereupon he spoke at a sparsely attended graveside centennial commemoration at Mount Herzl. While I was not present, it was through my friendship with Begin's chief of staff, Yechiel Kadishai, that I was able to obtain a transcript of Begin's heartfelt remarks. Before sending them, Kadishai had translated them into English. In 2012, I was contacted by Jabotinsky admirer and former president of North American Betar, Ronn Torossian. Torossian is the head of New York–based 5W Public Relations. He requested a copy of this landmark speech to share with the media.

In this impassioned graveside message, Begin addresses Jabotinsky directly. In my mind, I think of these words today as Begin's manifesto. It perfectly embodies his deep core beliefs emanating from his very soul and the vision he shared with Jabitonsky for the renewed State of Israel. I include the entire text below along with my interspersed comments:

Adoni, Rosh Betar,

Upon completion of the centennial of your birth – and this time only – we have come to address some remarks at your graveside. We report to you, Rosh Betar, that Jerusalem, the city that has become bound together, the eternal capital of Israel and of the Land of Israel, shall not be subjected to any division and is our liberated and indivisible capital and so it shall remain from generation to generation.

NOTE: Begin addressed Jabotinsky as the leader of Betar rather than as the leader of the Revisionist Party or the Irgun since it was through the youth group that Begin forged his close ties to Jabotinsky. Begin also notes, with the words "at this time only," the uniqueness of such a graveside address. Normally, offering comments at the grave of such a great orator would be viewed as presumptuous. But, since this was a centennial observation, a one-time exception could be made.

The western part of the Land of Israel is entirely under our control and it shall not be partitioned anymore. No part of this land shall be given over to a foreign administration, to foreign sovereignty.

We believe that a day will come when the two parts of the Land of Israel shall establish, peacefully, in agreement and understanding a covenant of alliance, a free confederation, for the purpose of joint cooperation, and then we shall see the fulfillment of the words:

From the abundance in our land shall prosper for the Arab, the Christian and the Jew.

NOTE: Begin underscores his and Jabotinsky's vision of a unified Land of Israel living in peace by citing the closing line of the third verse of The Betar Anthem. This poem, penned by Jabotinsky, was fashioned into a song that became the anthem of the Betar movement of my youth. It reflects the idea of a Jewish state existing on both sides of the Jordan River. The third stanza expands into a broad ideological vision in which everyone in Greater Israel will live in peace and dignity. The final verse ends with a religious oath taken from Psalm 137:5: "If I forget thee, O Jerusalem, let my right hand forget her cunning."

Begin's Labor Party successors, however, did appear to forget Jerusalem as they repeatedly gave back Israeli land in exchange for the false hope of peace.

We defend the dignity of Jewish people wherever they may be, since that is the basis for safeguarding the existence and future of our nation. We shall remember until the very last day of our lives and shall bequeath to our children after us, that those who arose against us in this generation to annihilate us, did not carry out their evil designs until they had succeeded in debasing our condemned people and depriving them of their human dignity.

We guard the security of our nation as the pupil of our eyes. Many are those who wait to entrap us. The path of tribulations has not yet come to an end.

We shall, however, ensure our national security with all the means at our disposal, with the heroism of our children, for whom you sang from the depths of your loving and believing heart:

Do not say that there is no more within us
The blood of our father, the Maccabee,
For three drops from him
Have been mixed into my blood.
When the enemy shall break from ambush,
We shall rise and we shall fight
Long live the youth: long live the sword,
Long live the Maccabean blood.

NOTE: *Begin again quotes from one of Jabotinsky's well-known poems, Ir Shalom or City of Peace.*

We will continue to pursue peace and to act by virtue of our inalienable right, for its realization; for wars are abhorrent to us, and the vision of eternal peace, conceived by the Prophets of Israel, the Prophets of truth and justice, dwells in our hearts and appears before us always.

We undertake a continuous endeavor in the rejuvenation of the Hebrew language, which today we and our children use fluently. It is beautiful in content, and not merely great in its expression, as you have taught us –

The most wonderful of all languages, the language of thousands of opposites, hard and strong as steel and at the same time soft and illuminating as gold; poor in words but rich in concepts; cruel in anger and living in ridicule as well as dainty in a mother's song at a time of comfort and conciliation.

It is a language whose voice often echoes like that of stones falling steeply from the mountain and often as the rumblings of grass in a spring morning. An unwieldy language, with bearlike fingernails and widespread wings of birds in flight.

The language of the Ten Commandments, and the song of Moses on the day of his death; the language of censure and the language of the Song of Songs; the language of David's lament and Isaiah's song of comfort; the language forgotten and unforgotten, already buried and yet living eternally.

We will continue to act for the promotion of social justice in the lives of our people so that there be light for Jew and Gentile together. The vision of justice, as we received it from you, Adoni Rosh Betar, is that poverty shall vanish from the face of the earth.

The return to Zion of most of the Jews from the West, the East, the North and the South is our aspiration, and it shall continue to serve as a beacon of light for our guidance.

We observe the ancient traditions of our people, the faith in the G-d of our fathers, since these are the sources of Israel's eternal existence.

One more message from our lips, Adoni Rosh Betar:

In those difficult days we saw you in your pain and suffering. We heard you calling our people, who did not wish to heed: Save yourselves, liquidate the Diaspora before the Diaspora liquidates you. In those days, on the threshold of those awful days, you told us, your pupils, your children: A day will come when our people will call upon you to conduct their affairs, to take responsibility for their future.

That day has come. To them, to your pupils, our nation in its state has again given the trust to bear the responsibility for assuring its liberty, its security, its peace, dignity, welfare and future, in the Land of Israel restored.

Blessed are the pupils, Adoni Rosh Betar, for whom a teacher like you arose and who continues to live in their hearts. Blessed be the teacher, whose pupils carry aloft his flag, believe in his vision and diligently fulfill his tenets."

NOTE: Just as Begin here blesses the memory of his teacher, I, likewise, bless Begin as my own. I am proud to call myself Begin's pupil and to carry aloft his flag, believe in his vision, and diligently fulfill his tenets.

—As translated and published with permission of Begin's former Chief of Staff, Yechiel Kadishai.

A number of groups have sprung up since Begin's death to preserve his legacy and to secure his place in history. The most prominent of these is the Menachem Begin Heritage Foundation, founded by a group that included me; its first director, Harry Hurwitz (1924–2008); Begin's chief of staff, Yechiel Kadishai (1923–2013); and Nate Silver (1921–1997), the national chairman of the Zionist Revisionist Organization of Canada. The foundation is headquartered in Jerusalem and operates the Menachem Begin Heritage Center, the official state memorial commemorating Menachem Begin, Israel's sixth prime minister. The center was opened in 1998 and is located on the Hinnom Ridge, overlooking Mount Zion and the walls of the Old City of Jerusalem. The center houses all of Begin's papers and serves as a learning center for students and historians. I am proud to serve as the president of the US branch of the organization, Friends of the Menachem Begin Heritage Foundation.

If this book piques your interest in the life of Menachem Begin and prompts you to visit the center on your next trip to Israel, I will consider having written it to have been a worthwhile endeavor indeed.

Chapter Seven

A Humble Heart

As I grew to learn more about the character of Menachem Begin, the overarching trait that most impressed me was the man's extraordinary humility. In this chapter I offer some glimpses and episodes that illustrate this admirable aspect of Begin's personality.

When Winston Churchill was told that his political rival, Clement Attlee, was a humble man, he responded with "No doubt he is, and he has much to be humble about." The same could NOT be said about Begin's humble nature. In the Jewish tradition, greatness and humility are not incompatible. In fact, they complement one another. The greater the man, the more humble he is expected to be. Begin certainly embodied this precept of humility. In fact, some might claim he was humble to a fault. If he boasted about anything at all it was his preference for the "simple things in life."

I recall discussing this aspect of Begin's personality after his passing with Yechiel Kadishai, who was his closest confidante. Yechiel shared a moment with me that took place a week after Begin had been inaugurated as prime minister. Begin called Kadishai into his office and asked him a question:

"Yechiel, tell me. Do I look any different now than I did a week ago?"

"No, you don't," came the reply.

53

"Then why do people treat me differently? I don't understand that."

"Because you're the prime minister," explained Kadishai. "You won the election. That's why."

The following incident likewise demonstrates both Begin's wit and his long-standing sense of humility.

Simona and I had just arrived in Israel and had come straight from the airport to Begin's apartment. As we entered, Begin stood up to greet us with open arms. Although this was not the sole reason, he was excited to see us because we would usually bring him books that he devoured at the rate of one per day. After kissing Simona's hand in his courtly manner and hugging us both, he bid us sit down.

"So, Hart, how did you get to Israel this time?" he asked. "Did you fly El Al?" When I replied that I had, he asked:

"I'll bet you flew first class, right?" he ventured.

"Actually, Simona and I flew business class."

"You know, when I used to travel by train around Europe before the war, I always went third class," he said, and then he paused.

"Well," he said finally, "aren't you going to ask me why I always rode third class?"

"Oh, yes, of course, Mar Begin," I obliged. "Tell me, why did you always travel third class?"

"Because there was no fourth class," he said with his characteristic broad smile.

I had witnessed Begin's humble nature before when he was a visitor in our home in 1976. We were honored that he had agreed to serve as the *sandak* (godfather) at the Brit Milah of our new baby, Josh. Begin was, at this point, the leader of the loyal opposition Likud Party in Israel. He had unsuccessfully run for the office of Israeli prime minister a total of eight times. As I invariably did, I introduced him to the group assembled in our living room as the next prime minister of Israel. I recall adding, "and Menachem Begin has always been my personal hero and idol ..." Begin said nothing to me at the time, but as soon as we were alone, he exploded.

"How dare you introduce me as your idol?" he said indignantly. "You worship idols? I'm not your idol! I don't believe in idols!" Judaism contains major sanctions against idolatry of any kind. I calmed him down by explaining that I was speaking figuratively, not literally, and that the audience fully understood it that way. I'm not sure he entirely accepted this explanation. I had clearly offended Begin's ingrained sense of humility and I never made that mistake again.

Begin's humility served him well as prime minister. In fact, as the following episode demonstrates, it was this characteristic that enabled him to successfully assemble a government coalition after his reelection to a second term as prime minister in August of 1981. While Begin's Likud Party had won the most seats in the Knesset, it had not won enough to constitute a ruling majority. Likud had captured only 43 of the 61 minimum seats required under Israel's parliamentary system. Begin was required to turn to the religious parties as he attempted to assemble a majority coalition.

As it happened, I was sitting with the prime minister, having tea in his office following his victory, when seven Haredi party leaders burst past Kadishai's outer office and loudly barged into the room. This behavior, with all the shouting, hand-wringing and arm-waving was nothing new and was considered politics-as-usual among the religious contingent. I recognized one of the leaders as Rabbi Menachem Porush, who was a Member of the Knesset from the Agudath Yisrael Party. He was joined by leaders of United Torah Judaism and other smaller parties of the religious right.

The rabbis were there to negotiate their requirements and conditions with Begin. Conditions they loudly demanded be met before they would agree to join the government. I wasn't exactly sure what specific points they were shouting about, but I was able to pick up several phrases being yelled repeatedly: "We will NEVER agree to that!" "No way! Not a chance! Forget about it!"

The prime minister and I were seated around the coffee table as I looked over to observe his reaction to this rowdy intrusion. He said nothing, and his face remained placid and unemotional. The rabbis circled around us and continued for many minutes shouting their demands as well as occasionally shouting at one another. Begin said nothing and remained stoic and serene in the face of all this tumult. He sat and listened as their voices rose to a crescendo. At this point several members of the contingent stopped to take a breath and the commotion abated for a split second. Begin grabbed the opportunity to address the men softly and calmly. He spoke to them in Yiddish— something he rarely did in public. I shall never forget his words:

"Raboisi. Hot men schoin gedavent mincheh?" which means: "Gentlemen. Have you already recited *Mincha*?" Mincha is a prayer

service carried out daily by observant Jews, typically shortly before sunset. Since this was around 3:00 p.m., it was not surprising that none of the rabbis had yet done so. Begin's question stopped them in their tracks. They immediately ceased their histrionics and looked at each other while shaking their heads no. Begin motioned with his arm and said in Yiddish:

"Nu, du iz di vant," which means, "So, there is the wall." Whereas in the rest of the world Jews are able to face the Temple Mount easily when they pray by always turning in the same direction (in America, Jews turn to the east), in the city of Jerusalem, it's not so easy. The direction you are required to face depends upon where in the city you find yourself relative to the Temple Mount.

In order to conduct a prayer service, a *minyan* (a quorum of ten or more Jews) is preferred. With the prime minister and me serving as numbers eight and nine, we were one person short. Begin turned to me and said: "Call in Yechiel and then we'll have a minyan." I opened the door and summoned Yechiel Kadishai, who joined us and made up the full complement as we launched into prayer.

After completing the *Mincha* service, the rabbis—now in a more moderate mood—began negotiating with Begin about the terms of their joining the coalition. I realized that it was not appropriate for me to be present for such discussions, so I said my good-byes and went back to my hotel. Although I was not present for the outcome of the negotiations, I read in the *Jerusalem Post* the following morning that the religious parties had agreed to join the coalition, and thus Begin was successful in establishing a new ruling government.

Begin could have easily responded to the raucous situation in his office as any other political leader might have done: by trying to out-shout the rabbis and scolding them for their unruly behavior. He opt-ed not to do that, and instead he changed the subject. This was a brilliant maneuver. Begin's sense of humility would not allow him to meet fire with fire. Instead, he responded to the scornful shouting of these leaders of the religious right with due respect and humble grace, and this act served to impress them and to disarm them.

There was another encounter involving the extreme religious right during Begin's term in office that likewise displayed his presence of mind and his humble nature. It was during my tenure as president of the Herut Zionists of North America, in July of 1977, that the prime minister agreed to speak at a sold-out luncheon we hosted at the Waldorf Astoria in New York. This was Begin's first visit to the US as Israel's head of state, and before heading to Washington to confer with recently elected US President Jimmy Carter, Begin had stopped in New York to pay his respects to the spiritual leader of the Chabad movement, the Lubavitcher Rebbe, Menachem Mendel Schneerson.

Begin's appearance at our event had received a good deal of press, and as a result, a noisy contingent of Jewish protesters had assembled across the street from the hotel brandishing anti-Israel signs and banners.

If you are unfamiliar with the Hasidic sect known as the Satmar-er, it may surprise you to learn that a group of religious Jews was protesting a public appearance by the prime minister of Israel. Ultra-Orthodox groups such as the Satmarer Hasidim and the Neturei Karta perceive Zionism and the establishment of the secular State of Israel as an anti-messianic act, conceived and born from sin. They vigorously deny the very legitimacy of the political return to Zion and do not recognize the sovereignty of the modern State of Israel. They believe that Jews are required to wait for a complete, miraculous, supernatural redemption of the land that can only take place at the coming of the *Mashiach* (Messiah) as described in biblical prophecy. They regard any attempt to establish a Jewish nation prior to the arrival of the *Mashiach* to be an aggressive aspiration to overstep human boundaries into the realm reserved for G-d. Such beliefs cause the Satmarer to make common cause with enemies of Israel.

On this day, the Satmarer demonstrators were armed with outrageous picket signs reading "Down With Israel!" "Down With Begin!" and "Free Palestine!" They were vociferously venting their wrath against the "unholy" Jewish state by shouting offensive epithets directed at Begin and the Israeli government. I had seen these folks before, and though I did not do so on this occasion, I had, in the past, confronted these bums face-to-face.

"Go home," I would shout back to them in Yiddish. "Why are you here? You're making Jews look like fools. You want to go back to a time when there was no Israel? When they took us to the gas chambers in cattle cars? Is that what you fools are demonstrating about!?" But my words would fall on deaf ears.

Shortly before the start of our event, I was called upon to join a delegation to accompany the prime minister from his hotel room to the ballroom. Our group took the elevator up to Begin's floor, collected him, and escorted the prime minister back to the elevator. As soon as we reached the ground floor and the elevator doors opened, the screeching of the Satmarer could be heard emanating from across the street. A member of our delegation (who shall remain nameless) began profusely apologizing to the prime minister for this disturbance.

"Oh, M-m-mister Prime Minister," he sputtered. "We are so sorry for this noise. It's those Satmarer causing all this trouble. I regret you are forced to listen to all of this." The gentleman went on until Begin raised his hand to stop him.

"There's no need to apologize," Begin said calmly. "That doesn't bother me in the least. In fact, I wish to tell you something." At this point he stopped and looked at the Jewish leader who had offered the apologies.

"It doesn't bother me at all that they are doing what they are doing," he repeated. "Because, I can assure you that their grandchildren will be Jewish and I am not so sure about your grandchildren."

What Begin did not know at that point was that the man he was addressing was, in fact, married to a non-Jewish woman and already had non-Jewish grandchildren. Later that evening, I pointed out this fact to the prime minister.

"Mar Begin," I said. "When you told the fellow that the Satmarer will have Jewish grandchildren but you weren't sure if he would be able to say the same thing, did you know that you were right?" Begin was dismayed at this news.

"Had I known this at the time, I would not have said such a thing." he replied. He felt remorse that he had inadvertently embarrassed the man, while his intention was to do the opposite. He wished to put the man at ease by explaining that no apologies were necessary. It was part of Begin's humble nature to invariably downplay his own celebrity status and to make sure those around him understood that he was no pompous big shot—but rather a simple Jew and a passionate Zionist.

On August 14, 1983, I had the *zechut* (privilege) of being asked by Israel Bonds leader David Hermelin to introduce Prime Minister Begin as he delivered what turned out to be his final public address before he resigned. Of course, we were unaware of this fact at the time. The occasion also happened to correspond with Begin's seventieth birthday. The audience was made up of four hundred Israel Bonds leaders assembled from around the world for a keynote address in the Chagall Hall of the Knesset in Jerusalem. In my remarks I mentioned how Begin had been my hero since I was 15 years old during a time when Jews were homeless and helpless. I gave him credit for kicking the British out of Palestine and his critical role in the founding of the State of Israel.

As Begin stood to speak after my intro, many were struck by his appearance. I could see that he was pale and looked decidedly frail for the first time. While his speech was labored, his message was a resounding one. His first words indicated that despite his appearance, his wit remained intact.

"Hart, you overdid it with that introduction. But, since it came from the 'Hart,' I gladly accept your praise and kind words." He smiled gamely as he punned my name. He closed with the following inspiring words:

"Remember, my dear friends, our people suffered much, lost many, won the day; nobody gave us our freedom. We had to fight for it, to redeem it, to give for it sacrifices, to defend it. All of us without exception of party affiliation, and we won. Why? Because our cause is just. So take note, my dear friends, and when you meet your friends, tell them so. There is a rule, unchangeable. The just cause will always win the day."

A few weeks after these words were delivered, Begin resigned his office and withdrew from public view for the remaining nine years of his life. He did not reveal his plans to anyone, although looking back, I can discern a dropped hint of his intentions during our visit to his office on the following day. Simona and I were on our way to the airport and had stopped off to say good-bye.

"Hart," he said, "you did such a fine job last night. Thank you for introducing me in such a wonderful manner."

"It was my honor, Mar Begin," I replied. He also thanked us for the beautiful historic artifact, an ancient water jug, which was presented to him as a birthday gift during the previous night's event. What he said next surprised me a bit and should have tipped me off:

"But you know, Hart, I'm seventy years old today. I'm getting to be an old man."

"Mar Begin," I protested. "What are you talking about? Seventy is not old. President Reagan is now seventy-four, and everyone knows he's getting ready to run for reelection."

"Well, Hart," he said dismissively, "Reagan is a *gezunter goy* (healthy Gentile)." I laughed and came right back with:

"But you're a *shtarker Yid* (strong Jew)!"

Begin laughed and said: "No, my friend. I'm seventy and I feel every bit of it."

Despite this friendly exchange, I left his office with no inkling of his intention to resign. Simona and I had noticed that he did appear more withdrawn and not as gregarious and outgoing as in the past, but we did not see what was coming. The announcement of his resignation caught us, along with the rest of the world, by complete surprise. I remember receiving a phone call at the time from Gabe Cohen, the publisher of the *Jewish Post & Opinion* newspaper.

"Hart, you just got back from Israel. Didn't your good friend Menachem Begin tell you he was going to resign?" I had to admit that he had not, although I mentioned the hints that he had dropped and our discussion about Reagan. I did not wish to quote him exactly, so I paraphrased Begin as responding with: "Your president is a 'robust individual,'" replacing the actual term *gezunter goy* with something a bit more politically correct.

Thinking back after digesting the news of his resignation, I recalled that Begin had spoken to me, on more than one occasion, of his intention to retire when he reached age seventy. I soon understood that this decision was yet another manifestation of the man's unsurpassed humility. A humility that extended beyond his term in office and even beyond his lifespan.

After Begin left office, he withdrew from public life and chose to spend his days living simply and reading the books we would frequently deliver to him. Many times I was asked by reporters and others who were aware of my friendship with Begin about the real reasons for his decision to go into seclusion. Was it because of the loss of his wife? Did he feel guilt over the casualties during the Lebanese War? My own opinion is that he was simply burned out. He had endured worldwide attention and fielded hundreds of phone calls per day for decades. The weight of being Menachem Begin every day had become a monumental burden. He was exhausted and drained and decided to withdraw completely from the public arena.

It was Begin's humility that prompted him to forgo the trappings of a former head of state after leaving office and instead relegate himself to a life of self-imposed seclusion. Since he treasured our close friendship, Simona, and I were afforded the unique opportunity to broach his wall of solitude and visit him in his private quarters during those years. At one point, we became concerned that this emotional isolation was having a deleterious effect on the man.

Simona and I found ourselves in Israel in May of 1985. I received a phone call at our hotel from Yechiel Kadishai, who had continued serving as Begin's closest aide after he had left office.

"He's asking about you," Yechiel said. "He wants to know if you are bringing him some books from America. How soon can you be here?" I said we would come right over. When we arrived, Yechiel met us and ushered us in.

Simona and I entered the apartment and sat in the living room, waiting for Begin to emerge from the bedroom. But he did not come out. We waited for about thirty minutes and he still failed to join us. I knocked on the bedroom door and received no answer. Perhaps he had fallen asleep, I thought, so I told Simona, "Let's wait a little longer."

After about ten more minutes, I said to Simona: "I know he's in there. Why don't you give it a try?" She agreed and knocked on the door. No answer.

"You know what?" I said. "Just go on in. Open the door and walk in. You used to be a doctor's assistant. It's okay." Simona did as I asked and found Begin sitting up in bed, wearing a bathrobe and reading calmly.

"He's okay," Simona relayed, and I followed her into the bedroom. He looked pale and withdrawn, but otherwise appeared to be in good health.

"Have you been out of bed today?" Simona asked.

"No. Not yet today, Simonelleh *(sih-MON-el-leh),*" he replied. He always addressed her with the affectionate diminutive, Simonelleh.

"Okay, Mar Begin, today we're getting out of bed. Let's go," she said. Simona was never awed or intimidated by anybody, including the former prime minister. She spoke to him plainly, like a member of the family.

"Naw, I don't feel like it. Not today, Simonelleh," he whined.

"No, no, no. We're going to walk around a little. It's not good for you to stay in bed all day," she insisted. Simona assisted him out of bed and offered her support as he began walking out the door and back and forth around the apartment.

Whenever we were in town, Simona took charge of his care. She advised his cook not to serve his meals in bed. "He should come to the table to eat," she instructed her unequivocally. Begin would hear such directives and chide Simona:

"Simonelleh, what do you want from me? Who are you? Napoleon?" he protested.

"Mar Begin," I responded. "What have you done? My mother calls Simona 'The General' and now you've made her 'The Emperor!' You've promoted her, and I have to live with her."

Our proactive style of care for Begin did not sit well with his family. His son, Benny, would tell me: "Just leave him alone. Don't bother him. He's a grown adult."

"That's the worst thing you can do," we told him. "You're wrong. You have to force him to get out of bed and to interact with people—even if it's just for short periods each day." Maybe we were overstepping our bounds, but I had seen this type of behavior among my nursing home patients and I knew that if they were simply left to themselves, they would fall into deep depression and eventually wither and die. We did not wish to see this happen to our friend.

Begin's mental attitude appeared much improved by our next visit. We were again met at the door of his apartment by Yechiel Kadishai.

"He's dressed up today," Yechiel whispered. "He's expecting his girlfriend later."

"Girlfriend?" I responded quizzically.

"Yes. Jeane Kirkpatrick," he said, referring to the former Reagan foreign policy advisor and the first woman to serve as the US ambassador to the United Nations, where she was an outspoken pro-Israel advocate. Begin and Kirkpatrick had gotten acquainted in March 1983 when she delivered a message of support from President Reagan to the Third International Conference on Soviet Jewry in Jerusalem.

Over time and, I believe, thanks to our efforts, Begin did start to open up a bit more. He would meet with us in the living room and he appeared to be his old self. He was always on top of the latest news developments and he would comment to us about the events of the day. "Shamir handled that pretty well" or "Reagan should not have gone there," referring to the US president's controversial visit to the Bitburg cemetery where German SS officers were buried.

Menachem Begin died in the early morning hours of March 9, 1992 at age 78. His funeral was a final testimony to the enduring humility of the man. His body was carried four kilometers from the Sanhedria Funeral Parlor to the Mount of Olives in a procession composed of tens of thousands of mourners. This fact is noteworthy because, as a former prime minister of Israel, Begin was entitled to a state funeral that would afford his grave a place of honor alongside other leaders of the state on Mount Herzl. Instead, and in accordance with his expressed wishes, recorded in a brief letter addressed to Yechiel Kadishai, Begin had asked that he be buried near the graves of his heroes from the underground, Meir Feinstein and Moshe Barazani on the Mount of Olives.

Barazani was a young Kurdish member of Lehi (Freedom Fighters of Israel, aka the Stern Gang) who had been captured by the British and was being held at the Central Prison in Jerusalem's Russian Compound. There he met his cellmate, Irgun fighter Meir Feinstein, who like Barazani had been sentenced to death. In the early hours of April 21, 1947, shortly before they were scheduled to be hanged at 4:00 a.m., the two cellmates peeled open an orange that had been smuggled into the prison. There they found an improvised explosive grenade. They waited until the guards were safely out of range and the two embraced each other tightly with the live grenade lodged between them. Their deaths—carried out in exception to traditional Jewish sanctions against suicide—made them eternal martyrs of the Israeli underground.

Begin's choice to be buried simply alongside the young heroes, rather than in the lofty heights beside the nation's celebrated leaders, represents a final example of the enormous and admirable humility of the man I am proud to call my personal hero.

Chapter Eight

The Fourth Estate

The term "fake news" was popularized during the Trump adminis-
tration in order to point out the bias that remains so prevalent in the
mass media. But this was not a new phenomenon. In fact, I first
heard the term decades earlier in reference to news coverage about
Menachem Begin. In this chapter I discuss the struggles with the me-
dia that were faced by Begin as well as by his successors. Struggles
during which I was occasionally able to offer some assistance.

It was in 1990, about six years after Menachem Begin had left office and gone into a self-imposed seclusion, that Simona and I happened to catch a segment on CNN. It was a bit of Middle East coverage by a new rising-star commentator named Wolf Blitzer. Blitzer had recently joined the network as its military affairs reporter and would soon cut his teeth on his coverage of the US-Iraqi conflict known as Operation Desert Storm. Exposure that would succeed in making his a household name.

Blitzer was describing former Prime Minister Begin's situation in a decidedly unflattering fashion. I don't have the exact transcript, but his words went something like this:

"Israel's former prime minister, Menachem Begin, is living un-der pitiful conditions these days. He lives alone in Jerusalem, bedrid-den and cut off from the world, in a windowless apartment and with no one to care for the 77-year-old former world leader."

Upon hearing this completely inaccurate description, Simona exploded.

"What!?" she exclaimed. "What is this guy talking about? Has he been there? I've been there, and I know his bedroom has a window and that he has a beautiful balcony. He doesn't live alone. He lives with his daughter, Leah. And he comes out every day. Especially when I'm there. And he has a cook and a housekeeper and whatever else he needs. How dare he say such a stupid thing. He doesn't know what the hell he's talking about. This is nothing but fake news!"

A few months later Simona and I found ourselves in the dining room at the King David Hotel in Jerusalem. As I was enjoying my breakfast, I saw Simona's eyes widen and her face twist into a steel-jawed grimace.

"It's him," she snarled from between clenched teeth. "It's that Big Bad Wolf guy from CNN." I turned around and watched as Blitzer and a few colleagues were being escorted to their seats at a nearby table. When I turned back I saw Simona rising from her chair.

"I'm going to go over there and raise some hell with this guy for what he said about Mar Begin." I could tell that Simona was on the warpath and, while I shared her outrage at Blitzer's junkyard journalism, I felt that discretion was the better part of valor in this case. I stopped Simona and convinced her not to go after Blitzer. I was genuinely afraid she might decide to pop him in the nose.

"Sit down, dear," I said, and she complied. "Someday I'll write all this down in a book and the world will find out the truth about Begin's situation."

That truth includes the fact that Begin, far from being the Alzheimer-afflicted wreck depicted in the popular media, invariably would demonstrate his keen mind and sharp wit during his retirement years whenever our little group regularly convened at his apartment on Saturday afternoons. I recall and still chuckle today as I think back to some of the jokes he would regale us with. Here's an example:

Our Shabbat group that day consisted of the former prime minister, Harry and Freda Hurwitz, Nate and Lil Silver, Yechiel and Bambi Kadishai, Haim Corfu and, of course, Simona and me. Our conversation turned to a personality in the news. Someone in the group pointed out that he was a *yekke*. *Yekke* is a somewhat pejorative term used to describe a German-speaking Jew who places great emphasis on efficiency, precision, and detail. The comment prompted Begin to turn to me and ask:

"Tell me, Hart. Do you know what it means to be a *yekke*?"

"Yes, I do," I replied.

"Now, let me tell you what a *yekke* is. I'll tell you with a story," he said, leaning back a bit in his chair. "It seems that there were three prisoners in the Bastille who were about to be executed. The trio, an Englishman, a Frenchman, and a *yekke,* were brought to the prison courtyard, where a guillotine stood on a platform. The executioner first asked the Englishman which way he wished to be positioned in the guillotine—face up or face down? The Englishman chose face up and was so positioned as the heavy blade was released. By some miracle, the blade stopped short one quarter inch above the prisoner's neck. Deciding that this was fate at work, the jailer released the

71

Englishman and allowed him to go free. Next, the Frenchman was asked the same question. Once again, he responded in the same way. Face up. Once again the heavy blade was loosed and once again it stopped just short of the Frenchman's neck. He was likewise pardoned by the jailer. Finally, the *yekke* was asked his preference. Face up or face down? He said: 'I won't tell you until you fix this thing.' That, my friend, is a true *yekke*."

As you can see, Begin had a wonderful sense of humor. As such, he liked to surround himself with witty people like his right-hand-man, Yechiel Kadishai, who likewise knew how to share a good joke. Kadishai was particularly adept at applying amusing monikers to certain people. His disdain for pretentious intellectuals was well known. "Do you know the definition of an intellectual, Hart?" he asked me once. I again played along and answered in the negative.

"It's someone whose education has exceeded his intelligence."

I recall standing next to Yechiel at a black-tie reception when we were approached by such an overly-educated fellow who shared a litany of complaints about Begin's domestic policies. As he walked away, I whispered to Yechiel: "Oy. What a *nudnick*!"

"Not exactly, Hart," Yechiel offered with a sly grin. "He's a Phudnick."

"*Mah zeh* (What's that)?" I asked in Hebrew.

"A Phudnick. That's a *nudnick* with a PhD." I doubled over in laughter and have used the term many times in the years since then—and I think of Yechiel each time I do.

Yechiel's wit endured to the very end. I recall a conversation we had a few months before his death at age 90 in 2013. We were lamenting the fact that the chairman of the Senate Foreign Relations Committee, an outspoken critic of Israel, John Kerry, had just been named by President Obama to succeed Hillary Clinton as secretary of state in Obama's second-term administration. We both agreed that Kerry had little understanding of Israel's security needs.

"The man is a perfect idiot," I stated emphatically.

"No, Hart," Yechiel corrected. "Nobody's perfect."

During Begin's second term, the press seemed to focus on his imperfections with increasing severity. It was, I believe, his desire to shield himself from the Israeli and American media—media that had treated him very harshly throughout his political career—that contributed to Begin's decision to go into seclusion. I respected this desire on his part and only once encouraged him to set aside his rule of not speaking to reporters. While my urging did temporarily arouse Begin's anger at me, I feel that the eventual outcome was a positive one. Let me explain.

In 1986, Begin's successor, Likud Party leader Yitzhak Shamir, was running for prime minister in a close race against Shimon Peres. Begin's endorsement of Shamir, were he to extend it, was regarded as being a big enough factor to influence the outcome of the election. True to form, Begin refused to issue such an endorsement or a statement of any kind about the impending election. He was out of politics and had nothing to say to the press that had shown him so much contempt over the years.

Begin's son Benny, Kadishai and others had all pleaded with Begin to agree to an interview with the press. All to no avail. On the day before the election, I was asked by the party leadership to speak to him and see if I could somehow prevail upon Begin to offer a last-minute public word of support for Shamir. As I sat in Begin's living room, I reviewed with him the importance of his endorsement for the future of the party and the country. The discussion became a bit heated after he turned me down flat.

"I know all this already, Hart," he said firmly. "The answer is no." I decided to try a new tack.

"I think I know why you've gone into seclusion and why you refuse to speak with the press, Mar Begin," I stated.

"Oh, you do?" he questioned skeptically.

"Yes. I believe you've taken a vow. A *neder*," I said, using the Hebrew word for oath. "I think you've made a vow to yourself to withdraw from the world. A vow that you cannot break. You have, for whatever reason, decided to go back into the state you found yourself in back at that Siberian prison. Completely alone and cut off."

I could see his displeasure welling up inside of him. But I wanted to shake him out of his stubbornness, so I persisted.

"Mar Begin, with all due respect, I see you regressing back to that time in your life. But instead of the Russians, this time you are your own jailer. You are keeping yourself in solitary confinement." His features made it plain that he was not at all impressed with my armchair psychoanalysis.

"Oh. So now you're a psychologist, are you? You don't know what you're talking about," he said disdainfully. "Do you have any idea what a *neder* is? A *neder* is an oath sworn to G-d. Would I do such a thing? I would never take a *neder*. Don't ever say such a thing to me again!"

He completely rejected my conclusions out of hand. And yet, when a reporter phoned thirty minutes later, I heard Begin, for the first time since going into seclusion, agree to take the call. I only heard one end of the conversation, but I assumed the reporter had asked if Begin supported Shamir in the election.

"What's wrong with you?" Begin responded brusquely. "Are you kidding? Of course I support Shamir." He went on to extend a solid endorsement over the phone, but to make it effective it had to come from Begin's own lips. Begin's nephew, radio news bureau chief Emmanuel Halpern, rushed over to the apartment with recording equipment. He succeeded in capturing Begin's endorsement on audiotape, but he was too late. By the time he returned to the studio to broadcast it, the moratorium on last-minute campaign advertising had gone into effect. Despite the fact that voters did not get to hear Begin's endorsement in his own voice, Shamir nevertheless won re-election. Shamir was, however, required to set up a national unity government, which saw him sharing the job of prime minister with Shimon Peres.

While I do not presume to take credit for Shamir's re-election, I do feel that my prodding of Begin contributed to his decision to relent and overcome his antipathy toward a hostile media and issue the critical endorsement.

Begin's treatment at the hands of the media had always been unfair and undeserved. His image during his long years as leader of Israel's opposition party ranged from that of a wild-eyed fascist guerrilla fighter to an out-of-touch old-world idealist wandering in the political wilderness. Both characterizations were completely wrong.

Unlike most of the Labor Party leaders, Begin shunned the open-necked, shirt-sleeved sabra look in favor of neckties and plain suits. He was also the first prime minister to take a *siddur* (prayerbook) and recite a prayer at the Western Wall upon assuming office. This somewhat pious persona reflected the value Begin placed upon Jewish traditions. Traditions that stretched back much further than the modern State of Israel. While the media mistook him for something of a throwback *shtetl* Jew, Begin, like Jabotinsky before him, was all about *hadar*. *Hadar* is a Hebrew word that literally translates to "splendor," but Jabotinsky, in his writings, expanded this meaning to encompass the values that he upheld through Betar and the Revisionist movement. In his usage, *hadar* embodies respect and a sort of beauty that generates dignity—an almost regal attribute. It is this broader meaning of *hadar* that Begin stood for and that, sadly, the press never understood.

While one might have expected that Begin's mistreatment at the hands of the press would have lessened after his surprising election victory in 1977, this did not prove to be the case, as the following account demonstrates.

The newly elected prime minister was introduced to the American public on the pages of its leading news source at the time, *TIME* magazine, in this way:

> "His first name means 'comforter.' Menachem Begin (rhymes with Fagin) has been anything but that to his numerous antagonists."

In addition to comparing Begin to Charles Dickens's stereotypical Jewish villain from the pages of *Oliver Twist*, *TIME* went on to pile on such negative appellations as "ruthless terrorist" and "dangerous fascist."

Despite Begin's numerous humanitarian actions during the first year of his term (e.g., rescue of the Vietnamese boat refugees, initiating the absorption of the threatened Ethiopian Jewish community, etc.), the media continued its relentless negative coverage. For example, the July 10, 1978, issue of *TIME* magazine was filled with coverage of the nascent peace feelers emerging between Israel and Egypt that would, in September, blossom into the Camp David Peace Accords between the two longtime adversaries. I had, by this time, canceled my subscription to *TIME* magazine, but I was directed to have a look at a personality profile sidebar about Prime Minister Begin in that issue that was authored by the Jerusalem bureau chief, Donald Neff. I could not believe what I read.

Neff began by assaulting Begin with a litany of unflattering descriptors such as "guerrilla leader," "ultranationalist," "inflexible," "myopic," and "deceptive." Some terms, like "truculent," sent me rushing to the dictionary. After this initial invective, Neff then stated that Begin, since assuming office, had caused all the worst fears of his critics to come true. He then incredibly proclaimed that "Begin, more than any other man, has set back the chances for peace in the Middle East." Understand that he wrote these words about a man who would, within four months, be awarded the Nobel Peace Prize for bringing about—more than any other man—peace in the Middle

East. It is hard to imagine how any statement could possibly prove more inaccurate.

The balance of the "hatchet job" piece went on to include a string of ad hominem attacks and petty, vindictive insults emanating from US State Department hacks. Neff closed by casting unfounded aspersions about Begin's health and delivering the "good news" that the man is probably too ill to serve out his full term.

Who in the world was this Neff writing about? This was not the Begin I knew. This was not the highly principled Zionist patriot and hero I had admired since my teens. The man Neff was describing was some sort of fabricated fiction invented to conform to the narrative being pandered by the media. I rushed to compose and fire off a response in which I vented my outrage and attempted to correct the dire misrepresentations that filled Neff's article. While it was heavily redacted, I was gratified to see that my letter, along with two others disputing Neff's character assassination, were printed in the July 24, 1978 issue:

> Your article "Begin: 'Beyond the Pale'" was the most vicious, vitriolic, venomous type of "reporting" I have ever read.
> The truth is that Mr. Begin is a Jewish patriot, honest, compassionate and peace-loving, as are the majority of Israelis who support him and are pleased with his leadership.
>
> *Hart N. Hasten*
> *Indianapolis*

I later learned that Donald Neff was an outspoken and antisemitic opponent of not only Begin, but the entire State of Israel. He went on to author a series of outlandish anti-Zionist books, including one that claims that "the Jew, Henry Kissinger," secretly headed a cabal whose mission was to turn US policy in favor of Israel. In another of his twisted treatises he openly laments the fact that Israel was not totally destroyed during the 1967 Six-Day War.

It was a sad reality that attacks such as this one did not cease when Begin withdrew from the public arena in 1983. The Western media continued its unfair treatment of the Israeli political right even as Begin's successor, Yitzhak Shamir, took over as prime minister.

I had first met Begin's successor when he was serving as the Speaker of the Knesset. Shamir was known as a dedicated and highly capable leader and had served as one of Begin's comrades in arms during the struggle for Israeli independence. Shamir had been the chief of the Lehi underground detachment, also known as the Stern Gang, during the British Mandate. Begin had great respect for Shamir and had always envisioned him as his successor. Shamir recognized that Begin's work as prime minister was going to be a hard act to follow and decided to adhere closely to Begin's policies. In so doing, he won the admiration of many both inside and outside the party. But such a stance also earned him the contempt of the liberal left-leaning media.

The Intifada erupted during Shamir's turn in office and placed enormous stress on his leadership. Yitzhak Rabin was serving as minister of defense at the time and inflamed the situation when he was widely quoted boasting about how he would deal with the insurgent Palestinians: "We will break their bones!"

The Intifada was marked by intense street fighting pitting young Palestinians, armed with stones, against well-equipped Israeli troops assigned to quell the disturbances. But all was not as it seemed. It became clear that the Intifada was not so much a popular uprising of liberation as a finely orchestrated exercise in media manipulation. Under the direction of Yasser Arafat, the street fighters would put on daily performances just as soon as the television cameras were set up. Arafat himself was quoted at the time cynically remarking: "We are only a stone's throw away from achieving our goal."

Arafat, a student of the American civil rights movement, was early to understand the vast power of the new media phenomenon of CNN. He wisely recognized that by staging such scenes day after day, they would be transmitted around the globe and serve to build up enormous world sympathy for his cause. Every half hour, on the half hour, CNN would show how poor Palestinian kids were being beaten up by vicious Israeli soldiers. As the media campaign forged ahead, Israel, under Shamir's leadership, was coming under more and more stringent criticism from the international community.

Unfortunately, Israeli leadership was not as quick to understand the political power of global public relations. As the situation continued to worsen, I became increasingly concerned and decided to see if I could be of some help. I decided to make a special trip to Israel to try to lend a hand. Upon arrival, I requested and arranged for a meeting with the prime minister to specifically discuss this matter. After welcoming me into his spartan residence and exchanging greetings, Shamir bade me sit down. I got right to the point.

"Mr. Prime Minister, I'd like to talk to you about the Intifada," I began. "You've got to do something about this." Shamir was a pugnacious and compact man whose face bore a permanent frown due to his bushy brow. His eyes bored through me as I continued. "This is an either/or situation. Either you conduct this like a wartime action, or you walk away."

"What do you mean?" he asked.

"Number one, you do not permit the media to have such free access," I said. "You are getting pummeled in the press all around the world." Shamir retorted with the standard Israeli line.

"Hart, if we let world opinion determine our course, we would no longer have a state." I could see that I needed to explain some of the new realities to the new prime minister.

"Mr. Prime Minister, we're living in a new age. CNN and other cable news networks are feeding nonstop news coverage to the entire world 24 hours a day. They constantly need colorful news stories to grab the attention of their viewers. And the bloodier the better. Images of big Israeli soldiers clubbing poor little Palestinian children are exactly the type of thing they're looking for. They show these images over and over every half hour in every country in the world. Do you realize what's going on here?" Shamir looked a bit taken aback as he pondered my question for a moment.

"Yes," he said weakly. "Yes, we do know about this." But I did not believe him. I did not believe he had an inkling of how Israel was being depicted around the world. Israel, due to its many cumbersome bureaucratic regulations, had been slow to embrace cable TV. While I would soon begin a project to help remedy this situation, at this point most Israelis, including Shamir, were unfamiliar with CNN.

"If you understand the seriousness of the situation, Mr. Prime Minister, then I urge you to do something about it one way or another," I stated. He indicated that I should go on.

"Either you get tough or you walk away. For example, one thing you can do to squelch this thing, once the cameras are no longer filming, is mass arrest. You instruct the troops to surround a group of rioting kids and then haul them off in trucks to a detention center. You require that their parents come to bail them out after hitting them with a large fine. In our country a parent is legally responsible for the criminal actions of his minor child. If you do this here, these disturbances will come to a stop." Shamir said he liked this suggestion and agreed to discuss it with his military leadership.

"But whatever you decide to do," I urged him, "keep the media out of it. Keep them out of these areas entirely. You may suffer negative press reaction for a little while. They'll criticize you strongly for this, but after a week they'll forget about it. They'll understand that there are no more bloody scenes to be filmed here and they'll move on to some other more accessible trouble spot."

I left the meeting believing that I had gotten through to Shamir on the importance of maintaining Israel's public image in the world. His subsequent actions, however, demonstrated that he chose to only heed my advice about getting tougher with the rioters. He continued to permit full media access as the violence escalated. Israel continued to be depicted as a cruel oppressor and the rock-throwing Palestinian children continued to be labeled as freedom fighters for years to come.

When I share accounts of my dealings with Israeli political leaders, friends are often surprised by my level of access and my ability to be completely candid with them. They say: "These fellows have advisors at their beck and call. Why do they choose to consult with you?"

The fact is that for the most part, Israeli leaders, and particularly prime ministers, lead rather lonely lives. When they are not out in front of a crowd delivering a stirring speech, they often find themselves quite alone and cut off. They are surrounded by aides and advisors, all of whom have some sort of axe to grind. Other than their spouses, there's really no one who will extend an unvarnished opinion. I found, for the most part, that they welcome the opportunity of discussing the affairs of state with someone like me who has no agenda and who wants absolutely nothing from them in return. Begin in particular, as well as Shamir, Netanyahu, and Sharon all permitted me—no, they encouraged me—to speak my mind freely, and that's exactly what I did. That is why I had no reservations about looking Prime Minister Sharon in the eye and telling him "You look terrible on TV." If I sugarcoated my opinions out of some sense of deference, I would turn into just another yes-man sycophant and soon find myself rendered irrelevant.

It is wise to recall that Begin's personal hero, Ze'ev Jabotinsky, was among other things a member of the media. As a young man, he had worked as a journalist for the *Odesskiya Novosti* newspaper, where he wrote under the pen name of Altalena, the Italian word for seesaw or playground swing. The experience served to expose the young reporter to the fragile and tenuous status of European Jewry. Sadly, today's journalists appear more intent on closing people's minds than opening their eyes to the truth.

Finally, I am saddened to report that the situation has not improved regarding media bias against Israel. If anything, it has become more strident and narrow-minded. This is unfortunate, because just as I witnessed how the media failed to present an accurate picture of Israel's leaders back then, the public is receiving an even more politically distorted view of today's leaders.

As an example of how the biased coverage of Israel on the part of the mass media has only worsened in recent years, here is the cover of a 2010 issue of *TIME* magazine that proclaims "Israel Doesn't Care About Peace." Absolutely nothing could be further from the truth. I can attest to the fact that every Israeli leader I have met (and that's nearly all of them)—in fact, every single Israeli I have ever met—cared about or cares about peace more than anything else in the world.

Chapter Nine

The Spirit of '76

In my 2002 memoir book, I recount the time that Menachem Begin visited our home in Indianapolis and served as the godfather at our new son's Brit Milah. At the time the book was published, I felt it unwise to reveal a very significant event that took place shortly after the ceremony. With the passage of time, that concern has diminished, and in this chapter I discuss what transpired.

In 1975 Simona and I learned that we would once again become parents. At age 45 some might argue that I was too old to be fathering babies, but I disagreed. Having another baby energized both Simona and me and made our marriage an even happier one. On February 23, 1976, Joshua was born, and among the congratulatory messages we received, one originated from Begin, who was in the US for a visit. I immediately phoned him.

"Mar Begin," I said, "thank you for the good wishes. Is there any way for you to travel to Indianapolis next week for the Brit Milah? You would honor us greatly if you could serve as the *sandak* (godfather) for our new son." I was, of course, delighted when Begin agreed.

On the morning of the Brit, I greeted Begin at the airport. Riding back in my car, he commented with a smile as he peered out the window:

"I see you had the city put up some road signs in my honor," he deadpanned. "Begin 55 mph. Begin 60 mph. Very nice of them.

Thank you, Hart." I could see that his sense of humor had not been dulled by the last several weeks of constant travel. I asked him:

"Mar Begin, how long has it been since you spoke with your wife?"

"Oh, for several days. Why?" he said.

"Would you like to speak with her now?"

"Of course. What do you mean?" I reached for my mobile phone, which in 1976 was a true novelty, and asked him for the phone number. I got through immediately and handed him the receiver. He was touched by the gesture and shared his feelings with Alisa.

"I'm in Indiana with this good man. Such a good man," he confided in Hebrew.

We arrived at our home, and I escorted him upstairs to the guest room where he would be staying. He took the suitcase from me and immediately pulled out a very well-worn copy of the Tanakh, the Hebrew Bible, and placed it on the nightstand. I made a comment and he picked it up to show me. He explained that this was the Tanakh that he kept with him during his years of imprisonment in the Siberian gulag. He carried it with him wherever he traveled.

The Brit Milah ceremony was a lovely experience for everyone (except perhaps little Josh) and it served to create a bond between my hero and my son. Every time we would meet with Begin from that point on, he would ask about Josh.

"So," he would invariably inquire, "tell me about my godson, Yeshayahu Alexander." In another example of Begin's photographic memory, he never failed to accurately recall Josh's Hebrew name.

I took advantage of Begin's presence in our community to organize a parlor meeting a few hours after the Brit in our home. As the guests arrived, I stood before my fireplace bidding everyone to take a seat and once again introduced Begin to the group as the next prime minister of Israel. He proceeded to deliver a stirring, off-the-cuff speech that interwove biblical teachings with the topic at hand and the political situation in Israel. Begin next demonstrated his substantial oratorical skills as he spoke eloquently about the Tel-Chai Fund. Named for the burial place of Zionist hero Joseph Trumpeldor, the Tel-Chai Fund was established after the 1929 Arab riots in Palestine. It had served as the fund-raising arm of Jabotinsky's Revisionist Movement when, initially, funds were used to support Jewish defense in Palestine and to teach self-defense techniques to Jewish youth.

The cover of a booklet promoting the Tel-Chai Fund. ca. 1935.
The Rimon Family Collection.

Begin explained how the fund today was in need of money to retire outstanding notes dating back to 1948. At that time, money was borrowed to provide pensions for the widows and orphans of fallen Irgun fighters. While the families of slain Haganah fighters were receiving government pensions, the Ben-Gurion administration saw fit to ignore the needs of the Irgun families. So funds had to be raised via loans and from private sources. Begin was concerned that failure to repay these loans would result in the loss of the pensions and impose a hardship on the families dependent upon them.

Begin's impassioned pitch got through to the well-heeled crowd, including Clarence Efroymson. Clarence was a scholar and something of a black sheep of the family. He once told me that he had been "infected" with Zionism while living in Austria during the 1930s. Clarence contacted me when he heard that Begin would be in town, and I arranged a private meeting between the two. After their visit, Clarence presented Begin with a copy of a book that he had recently translated from the original Hebrew into English: Yehezkel Kaufmann's *History of the Religion of Israel* (Union of American Hebrew Congregations, 1970). This encounter proved fortuitous years later after Begin was elected prime minister. He and I were in Los Angeles attending a private Tel-Chai fund-raising luncheon at the home of national Israel Bonds leader Bill Weinberg. Begin inquired about the "fellow who translated the book." I explained that Clarence was back in Indianapolis, but I would be happy to phone him.

"Clarence, I have an old friend of yours here with me in Los Angeles," I told him once we got him on the line. "It's the prime minister of Israel, and he would like to speak with you. The prime minister just told me that he does not sleep well at night because he is constantly worrying about how to pay back the pension fund loans he discussed with you." They chatted for a few moments about Tel-Chai, and Efroymson indicated he would help out.

After returning to Indianapolis, I visited with Clarence and told him I was following up on his conversation with Begin.

"Clarence, the prime minister sends his regards and also sends you a message," I began.

"What's the message?" Clarence asked.

"He says that he's read one of your books and thinks you are a very good writer," Clarence smiled appreciatively. "He also says that you should now write something that will make you a *great* writer."

"And what might that be?"

"A check," I said with a grin.

Clarence smiled broadly and said: "Hart, we need to have a prime minister in Israel that's focused on his job, not up all night worrying about some 30-year-old debts. Here's a check, and I hope that it helps." It was a generous gift and it certainly did help a great deal.

Many years later, on June 25, 2006, I was asked to address a gathering at the Menachem Begin Heritage Center in Jerusalem. The event was the dedication of the center's archive section, which had been named for Begin's closest advisor and his wife, Yechiel and Esther (Bambi) Kadishai.

I noted in my remarks that it was during Begin's visit to our home in 1976 that I had first heard the name Yechiel Kadishai. In looking back, I realized that I had heard it in connection with a truly historic moment. I recounted how, prior to his election as prime minister, Begin had agreed to attend our son's Brit Milah, where he had honored us by serving as the *sandak*. I went on to say:

> After the Brit ceremony, Begin received a telephone call from Jerusalem. In my humble opinion this telephone call changed the course of not only Jewish history, but world history. On the telephone from Jerusalem was Yechiel Kadishai. This was the first time I had heard his name.

> I learned that on that call Yechiel had strongly suggested that Begin cancel his planned trip to Los Angeles, scheduled for the following day, and return immediately to Jerusalem. The reason for the change was that talks concerning new elections for the Knesset had begun. As his political advisor, Yechiel Kadishai was convinced that it was imperative that Begin return to Israel right away to direct the talks, and Begin did exactly that. He canceled his trip to Los Angeles and flew straight back to Israel.

It was during those post–Yom Kippur War years of the mid-1970s that resentment was rising among the Israeli electorate. This growing feeling that the war had been mishandled by Golda Meir and the Labor Party had, by 1977, led to a growing disenchantment with the Alignment government headed by Labor Party leader Yitzhak Rabin. Rabin was struggling with political scandals and beleaguered by party infighting with his political rival, Shimon Peres. Kadishai recognized this growing trend—as well as a shift to the right on the part of the National Religious Party—as a ripe political opportunity. He advised Begin that a chance now existed for the Likud Party to capture a critical number of additional Knesset seats and perhaps even secure the prime minister's office.

Begin seized the moment and flew home immediately. Once there, he began intensely campaigning across the country. Begin was successful in building widespread support among the Mizrahi community, composed of first- and second-generation Jewish refugees who had been expelled from Arab countries in 1948. This growing demographic was turned off by the secular-style Judaism being practiced by Labor Party leaders and found Begin's respect for traditional values highly appealing. Hence, a little more than a year after receiving that fateful phone call, Menachem Begin was elected the sixth prime minister of the State of Israel on May 17, 1977. Had he not complied with Yechiel's summons, received at our home the previous year, history may have taken a completely different turn.

As things turned out, Begin's election stunned the world. He had run for office eight times previously and lost. His victory represented a record for any candidate in a Western-style democracy. No one had ever lost so often and then managed to seize victory from the jaws of defeat. Begin's election signaled something far more than the elevation of a single man to a position of political power. It was, historians agree, a watershed moment in the history of Israel that saw the nation take a turn to the right and begin to move away from its socialist heritage. The term associated with this election in Israel is *mahapach*, which may be translated as "turnaround," but more accurately means "upheaval." An upheaval that got underway with a phone call from Kadishai to Begin on March 1, 1976.

I remember thinking, after the phone call was concluded, that this fellow Kadishai must be a very bright and astute individual. No wonder that Begin referred to him not as an aide, but as "my trusted friend," "my devoted companion," "my colleague," "my associate," and "my right-hand man."

That last appellation (right-hand man) served as the title of a book about Kadishai's life that was produced with my support by the Begin Heritage Center and Menachem Michelson in 2016 (Gefen Publishing House). In it, I am quoted as I describe the special relationship between Begin and his right-hand man:

> Begin valued Yechiel's sensible judgment. He trusted Yechiel's honesty, decency, and boundless loyalty. Begin knew that Yechiel would never exploit anything for his personal good. I never knew anyone else so dedicated to another person as Yechiel was to Begin. This was a love story that was hard to describe. As regards his character, when needed, Yechiel knew how to walk on tiptoe and how to be strict without shouting.

A few months after the Brit, I had the pleasure of meeting Yechiel and Bambi, and we quickly became close friends. My late brother Mark and I worked very closely with Yechiel in his capacity as the coordinator of Tel-Chai's fund-raising efforts. Some of the others with whom I was honored to work on this worthwhile endeavor included Nathan and Lil Silver, Yaakov Meridor, and Dr. Reuven Hecht. All of us were motivated by our deep respect for Menachem

Begin and not only solicited others but also provided our own financial support to the cause. Once Begin was elected prime minister, our task became measurably easier and we were eventually successful in retiring all of the Irgun's outstanding debts.

As mentioned, my remarks at the Begin Heritage Center took place in June of 2006. I had delivered an address there some two years earlier on the occasion of the facility's official dedication as a government-sanctioned visitor's landmark. This was a state occasion that saw Prime Minister Ariel Sharon as well as other high-ranking government officials in attendance. My remarks were preceded by those of Prime Minister Sharon, who spoke in Hebrew. I felt that presenting Begin as both the man I knew and admired—as well as a historic figure and statesman—would be the most appropriate way for me to proceed. I decided to speak in English.

I began by recounting, as explained in this book, just how I had heard of Begin when I was a Jewish refugee teenager in the DP camps and how he had become my hero.

> Years later when I finally met my hero in the flesh, I admired him even more. He became my friend, my teacher, my mentor, my role model. I admired his simplicity, his lack of pretense, and above all his unwavering integrity and honesty.

I then went on to make a unique comparison:

> In my mind, he was Israel's Abraham Lincoln. And with all due respect to Honest Abe, to me, Begin was an even greater leader than President Lincoln. After all, when it came to avoiding a civil war, Begin succeeded where Lin-

coln did not. Mr. Begin must also be credited with laying the foundation of democracy in Israel. He understood and valued democracy more than any other prime minister in the history of modern Israel.

This was no exaggeration on my part. A review of the early history of Israel will reveal that the newborn nation veered perilously close to civil war on several occasions. Had it not been for Begin's decision to exercise restraint by ordering his followers not to return fire as they were being attacked by Ben-Gurion's forces during the *Altalena* incident, many historians feel civil war would have erupted there in Tel Aviv harbor in 1948. There were also insurrectionary actions taken by supporters of Begin's opposition to the acceptance of German reparations in 1952. He recognized this threat and reluctantly accepted the decision of the democratically elected Mapai government, thereby once again averting a possible civil war.

Since making that speech, I have seen several similar comparisons surface. Some refer to Ben-Gurion as Israel's George Washington and label Begin as the nation's Abraham Lincoln. A look at the following two quotes underscores the validity of this Lincolnian comparison:

"Do I not destroy my enemies when I make them my friends?"

—Abraham Lincoln

"We must put [tragedies] behind us in order to establish friendship and make peace the beauty of our lives."

—Menachem Begin's Nobel Peace Prize acceptance speech

Chapter Ten

Alisa

While my friendship with Menachem Begin was certainly a special one, it must be understood that the closest and most significant relationship of his life was with his beloved wife, Alisa. In this chapter I offer my recollections of being with the prime minister when he received the devastating news of Alisa's death. I then share some background and personal reflections about this extraordinary "Woman of Valor."

L et me begin by stating that the episode I am about to recount represents what is probably one of the most traumatic experiences of my life.

It was during Menachem Begin's final visit to the US as prime minister that Simona and I found ourselves, on a Saturday afternoon, November 13, 1982, checked into the Century Plaza Hotel in Los Angeles. Begin was scheduled to deliver a major address before a large audience at an Israel Bond event that evening and we were there as part of his entourage. The Israeli contingent had taken over the entire nineteenth floor, where very tight security was maintained, while we, along with other Americans, were ensconced one floor below. I enjoyed free access through the security apparatus thanks to my lapel pin pass. At about 4:45 p.m., I walked up to the nineteenth floor, through the checkpoint, and was making my way toward Begin's suite when I was nearly tackled by Yechiel Kadishai. He grabbed me and quickly shoved me into an empty room.

"What's going on, Yechiel?!" I demanded.

"Where's Simona?" he said gravely.

"She went to visit her mother. What's the matter?" Simona's parents lived in Los Angeles.

"I just got off the phone with Benny in Jerusalem," he said, referring to Begin's son. "It's Alla. She's dead." Alla was the affectionate name by which Begin's wife, Alisa, was known to her close friends and family. I was stunned into momentary silence.

"Oh, no. What happened?" I finally managed to get out.

Yechiel quickly recounted what he knew about Alisa's death. I was aware of her long-standing struggle with asthma and emphysema. In fact, I had consulted with the family in the past about medications used to treat her condition. Yechiel then turned to the matter at hand.

"We have to tell Menachem," he said, looking me in the eye. "Benny gave me strict instructions that you and Simona must be in the room when we give him the bad news."

"Are you the one who is going to tell him?" I asked apprehensively.

"No, Dr. Gotsman will see to that," he replied, referring to the head cardiologist from Hadassah hospital, Dr. Mervyn Gotsman, who, because of Begin's heart condition, always traveled with the prime minister.

"You must keep this quiet," cautioned Yechiel. "Not even the security people know about this. No one can know until we inform the prime minister. Can you locate Simona quickly?" he asked.

"Yes, of course. I'll contact her right away." I reached Simona at her mother's home and she returned to the hotel within thirty minutes, but locating Dr. Gotsman was not so easy. He was an observant Jew and this was Shabbat. He had gone to pray at a small synagogue somewhere on Pico Boulevard. We were unable to reach him and had to wait nearly two nervous hours for his return. During this time we unsuccessfully sought out Begin's daughter, Leah, to inform her about the death of her mother. Once Gotsman arrived, we were assembled and ready to deliver the sad news to the prime minister. The tragic scene that followed will be etched into my memory for the rest of my life.

By now it was 6:30 p.m., and Begin had finished getting dressed for the evening. He was seated on the sofa wearing a tuxedo. Kadishai, Dr. Gotsman, Simona and I filed into the room and closed the door behind us. I could immediately tell from Begin's concerned expression that he sensed something was wrong. Dr. Gotsman stood before him and in hushed tones delivered the news that his beloved Alla was gone. Begin cried out as if wounded. As bitter tears welled up in his eyes, he kept repeating: *Lamah azavti otah*?" "Oh, why did I leave her?!" His lamentations were heartrending. "I should not have listened when she told me to go. She was in the hospital. I should have stayed by her side."

Simona tried to console him, "Don't blame yourself. The doctors told you that it was okay for you to go."

"Doctors! What do they know?" he muttered as he wept openly. I felt a twinge as I observed Dr. Gotsman listen to these less than flattering words.

The phone rang. Yechiel picked it up and said hello. "It's Benny again," he whispered to me.

"Benny, I'm so sorry about your mother," Yechiel said in Hebrew. "She was a great woman. Please accept our condolences." I asked Yechiel to convey our condolences as well.

Benny evidently asked to speak with his father. Yechiel looked at the prime minister and could see that he was completely overcome and in no condition to talk. "Maybe later, Benny," he said into the phone.

"He wants you or me to ask his father where they should bury his mother and then call him back," he reported. Yechiel turned and immediately broached the subject with Begin.

"Menachem, Benny wants to know what he should tell Haim Corfu about where Alla should be buried," he asked gingerly. Corfu was then serving as Israeli Transportation Minister and was also serving as the Herut Party's contact person for the *Chevra Kadisha* (burial society).

"The same place as me," came the curt reply. Yechiel's face showed puzzlement.

"I don't know where that is," Yechiel admitted.

"What do you mean, you don't know? Don't you remember? I gave you an envelope with my will in it when I was hospitalized in Ichilov." Yechiel strained to remember, and then recalled an envelope that Begin had entrusted to him and that he had placed into a small tin box that had held chocolates. He had put the box into a cubbyhole in his bookcase at home.

"But, Menachem," explained Yechiel, "I never opened the envelope."

"Of course, you're right," Begin said, realizing that he had always assumed that his own death would precede his wife's. "I wrote that when the time comes, you should bury me on the Mount of Olives next to the graves of my heroes." He was referring to the graves of the two captured Irgun and Lehi martyrs, Moshe Barazani and Meir Feinstein, who elected to commit suicide rather than face hanging at the hands of the British. Yechiel called back Benny, who relayed the message to Haim Corfu that his mother should be buried on the Mount of Olives, close to the graves of Barazani and Feinstein.

At this point Begin looked down and exclaimed: "Look at me. I'm in a tuxedo. Why am I in a tuxedo? Oh, yes, I'm supposed to speak somewhere tonight," he remembered.

"We've canceled your speech, Menachem," said Kadishai, taking charge of the situation, "and we're flying back home tonight. You should change into something more comfortable."

Yechiel turned to Simona and me and asked: "Will you help pack his suitcase and get him ready to go?" We naturally agreed.

We were hoping to inform both Begin and his daughter, Leah, about Alisa's death at the same time, but we were unable to locate her and decided to proceed. At this point, Leah entered the hotel room. She took one look, saw her father in tears, and demanded to know what was going on. We all stopped what we were doing and stood mutely, just looking at each other for an awkward moment. Leah peered into one face and then the next and finally shouted:

"Ima! It's Ima! Something's happened to my mother! What has happened? Someone please tell me."

I expected Dr. Gotsman to deliver the sad news to her, but he remained silent. I couldn't take it anymore. I walked over, took Leah's hand and bade her sit down on the sofa. I looked at her squarely and pulled no punches as I told her: "Correct. Your mother has died." I had faced this type of situation fairly frequently in the nursing home business and I learned that the direct approach is always the best way to deliver this type of news.

Leah was devastated, and now we had two distraught people to deal with and to pack for. After helping to organize Begin's suitcases, we walked toward Leah's room to assist her. On the way, I ran into national Israel Bonds leader Sam Rothberg, who had been waiting for some time to see Begin. I gave him the bad news and he asked that I pass on his condolences. By now, word was spreading quickly among the group that Alisa had died and that the prime minister was returning to Israel.

Yechiel then walked into the room and announced to us: "Benny would like for you and Simona to travel back home with us." We quickly agreed and went off to pack our own bags and prepare for the flight. We soon realized that we did not have our passports with us. Yechiel assured us that this would be no problem since we would be aboard the prime minister's plane and would not need to pass through customs.

By 10:30 p.m. we were all assembled on board as the eastbound military jet took off. Begin was stretched out on a cot behind a partition from which he would emerge from time to time. Simona prepared tea for him during the flight, but her major role was in consoling Leah. I believe that it was primarily for this purpose that Benny had asked us to come on board. He understood that Leah would take the news of her mother's death very hard and that Simona's presence would be a comfort to her. He was correct.

Over the ensuing years, Simona and Leah have developed a close friendship that has lasted to this day. Through her position with El Al Airlines during those years, Leah always seemed to be aware of our presence whenever we traveled to Israel and never failed to drop by for a visit.

The flight touched down in New York, where United Nations ambassador Yehuda Blum and his wife Marion came aboard to extend their condolences to the prime minister and his daughter. After taking on fuel, the plane took off again, arriving at Ben-Gurion airport at 1:00 a.m. The funeral was scheduled for later that day, and by now word had spread quickly throughout the country. What was to have been a private family funeral was soon swamped by thousands of Begin's admirers, wishing to pay their respects.

After the burial, Begin asked that we stay with him during the traditional seven-day mourning period. According to Jewish custom, during this time of *shiva* the mourner is to wear torn clothing and remain seated close to the floor. Simona and I frequently sat next to the prime minister during this period as he accepted the condolences from an unending stream of well-wishers, including top Israeli officials, respected rabbis, celebrities, ambassadors, and representatives from dozens of nations from around the world.

In a form of ancient cathartic therapy, Jewish tradition encourages a bereaved loved one to talk freely during the initial mourning period. Accordingly, we refrained from initiating any conversations and permitted Begin to speak uninterrupted about any topic he wished. And talk he did. Sitting in a torn shirt, he reminisced freely about such topics as his relationship with Jabotinsky, his time in a Soviet prison, and the birth of his children. But his recollections would always turn back toward his Alla. In this way, I believe he did manage to expiate his guilt over not being at her bedside at the end.

Each morning a crowd of men would fill the residence for the traditional prayers, donning the black leather *t'fillin* (phylacteries) and chanting the call and response prayers as Menachem and Benny Begin recited the Kaddish prayer in memory of their beloved wife and mother.

I had contacted my brother, Mark, and asked that he mail us our passports, which he did, enabling us to return to the States with no difficulty. We stayed in Israel for several weeks after the initial seven-day mourning period had concluded to offer what help we could. Both Benny and Leah thanked us for staying and said that our presence was a comfort to their father. We, of course, considered it an honor to console the prime minister of Israel as he grieved the loss of his cherished life partner.

•

At the time of her death, Alisa Begin was only 62 years old, and she and Menachem had been married for 43 years. She was known as a strong-willed, but publicity-shy, observant Jewish woman.

Alisa Arnold, along with her twin sister, was born into a well-to-do family in Drohobych, Galicia (today Ukraine), in 1920. Her father was in the oil drilling business and enrolled her in Hebrew school at age seven—something rare for young Jewish girls at the time. Her father was an active supporter of the Zionist Revisionist Party, and at age 14, Alisa joined Betar. While still a teenager, she met her future husband when he was a lodger in their home during one of his tours of the party's Betar branches.

Menachem and Alisa were married on May 29, 1939, in Drohobych. The wedding was attended by hundreds of Betar activists, with Revisionist leader and Begin's mentor, Ze'ev Jabotinsky, among the guests. Begin, who had received a law degree from Warsaw University in 1935, began teaching law classes at a nearby school. A few months after the wedding, on September 1, 1939, German forces invaded Poland, marking the outbreak of World War II. The prediction that Jabotinsky had been railing about for years was about to materialize. The diaspora had embarked on the organized destruction of the Jews of Europe.

The young couple fled when the war broke out and set out immediately on an unsuccessful attempt to reach the Romanian border. They traveled on trains that were bombed from the air, by wagon, and by foot with all their possessions in knapsacks on their backs.

After a march that lasted two weeks, the couple arrived in Vilnius, the free capital of Lithuania. In the summer of 1940 the Soviet Army entered the city and Begin was arrested for "Zionist activity." At this point Alisa set out to make *aliyah* (immigrate) to Mandatory Palestine.

Meanwhile, Begin was sentenced to eight years in a Siberian labor camp. He served one year of his sentence in the gulag and was freed under the terms of a British-Soviet-Polish understanding. The agreement called for Polish Army general Władysław Anders to establish a Polish brigade to fight alongside the Red Army against the Germans. Known as Anders's Army, the troops, composed mostly of Polish civilians who had, like Begin, been deported to the USSR from Soviet-occupied Eastern Europe, were evacuated in March of 1942 via the Persian Corridor through Iran, Iraq, and finally into Mandatory Palestine.

Hence, wearing a Polish Army uniform, Begin reunited with Alisa in May 1942, after which the couple was inseparable. The following year, Begin succeeded Yaakov Meridor as the leader of the underground Irgun Zvai Leumi (Etzel). As such, he was often required to disguise himself as a student, a rabbi, or a doctor in order to avoid arrest by the British authorities. Alisa accordingly posed as a *rebbetzen* (the wife of a rabbi) named Sassover, or as a Mrs. Konigshoffer, or assumed some other alias as the situation required.

During a four-day curfew in Tel Aviv, the British police searched from house to house for Begin and others on the Palestine "Most Wanted" list. Alisa maintained her composure during the searches while her husband hid in a false compartment built into the ceiling of their bathroom. Many years later, Begin shared some details about this harrowing episode. He was able to endure the claustrophobic confinement and the hunger, he said, but he suffered greatly due to his unquenchable thirst.

I recall how Begin's comrades from his underground days told me how Alisa could be very assertive in private and often kidded her husband. But she kept quiet at meetings of the underground high command that often met in their home. They told how, when Begin surfaced from the underground in 1948 and entered the Knesset, Alisa grew devoted to his political career. She became a fixture in the visitors' gallery whenever Begin spoke and was frequently seen lunching with him in the members' dining room.

When her husband won the premiership in 1977, he invited her to the stage during the victory celebration after introducing her with a passage from the book of Jeremiah (2:2): "I remember the kindness of your youth, the love of your bridal days, and how you followed me through the wilderness ..." At this point, instead of reciting the actual text, "into a land not sown," Begin substituted the words "into a land sown with mines," referring to the difficult period he went through when he fought in the Polish Army and in the underground against the British. Although I was not present at the victory celebration, I had the pleasure of hearing Begin introduce his wife in this manner several more times, including at the state reception following the signing of the Camp David Peace Accords in Washington in 1978.

Despite suffering from bronchial ailments throughout her life, Alisa accompanied her husband around the world after his election in her role as First Lady of Israel. This included numerous trips to the United States. I recall being told by Begin that, when she arrived with him on his first official visit, she refused to allow the Israeli embassy to fund the purchase of some new shirts for Begin. "By no means. The taxpayers will not pay for my husband's shirts," she proclaimed. Alisa likewise accompanied Begin to Stockholm when he was awarded the Nobel Peace Prize.

Alisa was known to dress simply, showed little interest in social life and, like her husband, was an avid reader. She zealously protected her privacy and refrained from being interviewed by the media. Like her husband, her most endearing quality was her genuine humility. Even as wife of the nation's head of state, Alisa used public transportation to get around Jerusalem and declined to use a government vehicle.

In 1982, Alisa's asthma became worse and her condition rapidly deteriorated. She was repeatedly hospitalized, occasionally being put on a ventilator. Billionaire Armand Hammer, who was a fan of her husband's, sent two international pulmonary experts to examine her. The treatment they recommended helped to extend her lifespan.

As per Begin's wishes, Alisa was buried on the Mount of Olives in November 1982, where ten years later, Begin would join her. She is remembered as a doting grandmother and a devoted mother to her three children: daughters Hassia and Leah, and Ze'ev Binyamin (Benny), a former government minister and New Hope Party Knesset Member.

My personal connection with Alisa grew out of her extensive volunteer activities for the disadvantaged, for which she was known and respected. Although known for her modesty, Alisa was not above using her influence and connections as the prime minister's wife to benefit the causes she believed in. For example, she contributed to the establishment of hostels and schools for people with disabilities and special needs and raised money for a variety of organizations involved in the field.

Alisa asked me to join the board of the Assaf Harofeh hospital, named after the "Jewish Hippocrates" and today known as the Shamir Medical Center, located outside of Tel Aviv. Just as I was pleased to work in behalf of the worthy projects to which Alisa was dedicated, she likewise offered her support for my pet causes. I shall never forget the warm note I received from her in 1980 after the prime minister had reported to her about a visit to our local Jewish day school. Alisa graciously wrote me the following letter in re-sponse *(see following page)*:

ALISA BEGIN

· Jerusalem, February 3, 1980

Mr. Hart Hasten
901 Roundtable Court
Indianapolis, Indiana 46260

My Dear Friend,

~~I write to you in your capacity as President~~
of the Board of the Indianapolis Hebrew Academy to
tell you how delighted I was to learn of the progress
of the school.

I sincerely believe the Hebrew Academy
to be one of the most important investments your
community can render unto itself, for your school
is a guarantee of the Jewish future. All of us who
care for that future know that there is no substitute
for a solid Jewish education, one that inculcates into
our children a knowledge of the treasures of our unique
and ancient heritage. The continuing growth of the
Hebrew Academy means that ever wider circles of the
Jewish youth of Indianapolis will grow up proud to be
Jewish with a love of Torah, of Zion and of the whole
Jewish people.

It is in this spirit that I send to the officers,
the staff and the students of the Indianapolis Hebrew
Academy my very best wishes from Jerusalem, our
eternal and indivisible capital.

Sincerely,

Alisa Begin

Finally, it was thanks to a unique role into which I was directed by Alisa Begin that I shall always remember her. Unlike most Nobel Prize winners, Menachem and Alisa Begin opted not to keep the six-figure prize money but instead to donate the funds to charity. To fully appreciate the singular significance of this gesture, it is important to realize that the Begins were not, by any stretch, wealthy people.

With the exception of the first female recipient, Marie Curie, who poured her winnings into further scientific research, other winners used the proceeds to enrich themselves—with the exception of Menachem Begin, who instead asked Alisa to distribute the money to worthwhile causes. She asked me to serve on a board to administer a philanthropic trust fund she had established to bequeath the Nobel Prize money. The fund was soon issuing grants directed primarily to worthy Israeli college students. Alisa herself sat on the review committee that approved these financial aid scholarships to bright and deserving young Israelis, enabling them to attend college.

Alisa realized that by providing advanced educational opportunities to Israel's talented young people, the Nobel Prize money was being used to ensure and sustain Israel's future. Nothing could be more of a tribute to the humility and legacy of Alisa and Menachem Begin than the accomplishments of today's generation of Israeli professional, business, and political leaders—many of whom received their training thanks to the far-sighted and magnanimous generosity of this exemplary couple.

The scholarship fund, today known as the Asper Fund, remains in existence and is administered by the Menachem Begin Heritage Foundation.

Hart N. Hasten

Chapter Eleven

Peacemaker

In the minds of most Americans, Menachem Begin is best known as the Israeli prime minister who forged the Camp David Peace Accords along with the Egyptian president, Anwar el-Sadat. Thanks to my special relationship with Begin at this point, I was afforded a ringside seat to the inception and development of this historic agreement. In this chapter, I share a few of those recollections..

B egin's election in 1977 caught the entire world by surprise. The entire world except for me, that is. Simona and I had wanted to be in Israel for the election, but were unable to make it. As we retired to our own Indiana beds on Israeli election night, with the outcome still undetermined, I said to Simona: "Tomorrow our friend will be the new prime minister of Israel." My prediction was not based on anything more than my own instincts and faith in the wisdom of the Israeli electorate. I just felt that this was his time, and I was delighted to awaken the next morning to discover I was right.

We rushed to Israel shortly after the election, and Begin greeted us for the first time in the prime minister's office. He made the comment that we would hear over and over again during the coming years: "Hart, you had more confidence in me than I had in myself," he said generously.

At our first meeting in the prime minister's office, Begin shared a dark moment that had recently taken place during the celebration reception at the King David Hotel marking his election victory.

"I spotted someone I've always wanted to meet," Begin said. Sir Isaiah Berlin was a Latvian-born British philosopher and world-renowned academician. "So I shouted to him: 'Isaiah, come over. I want to shake your hand. I'm so glad that you're here.'"

The noted intellectual's response to this invitation, Begin told me, was to turn his back and walk away. Begin was hurt by this public affront and never spoke to the man again.

"Berlin is one of those JWTKs," Begin later told me. By the puzzled look on my face, he could tell I did not understand.

" A Jew With Trembling Knees," he explained.

I heard Begin use this appellation often in describing those Jews he felt did not live up to the "blood of the Maccabees" that flowed in their veins. His most noteworthy use of the term occurred in June 1982 during his tenure as Israel's prime minister. Begin was in Washington testifying before the Senate Foreign Relations Committee headed by Democrat Delaware senator, and future president, Joe Biden. Biden was subjecting Begin to a harsh upbraiding over Israel's settlement policies, threatening to cut off economic aid to Israel unless he agreed to immediately cease all settlement activities. Begin responded with a resounding rebuke that could have just as easily been uttered today, some forty years later:

> Do not threaten us with cutting off your aid. It will not
> work. I am not a Jew with trembling knees. I am a proud
> Jew with 3,700 years of civilized history. Nobody came

to our aid when we were dying in the gas chambers and ovens. Nobody came to our aid when we were striving to create our country. We paid for it. We fought for it. We died for it. We will stand by our principles. We will defend them. And, when necessary, we will die for them again, with or without your aid.

With Begin's ascension, everything in the government was open to us. I enjoyed full access to his private office at any time—regardless of whom he happened to be meeting with. This entrée presented several amazing opportunities for me to enjoy a ringside seat to history.

I recall how, a few months into his term, Begin had run into the Romanian ambassador, Imre Kovacs, at the Israeli president's official residence. Shortly after this brief encounter, he summoned the ambassador to the prime minister's office for a conference. Kovacs was just walking out as I entered the room. As I sat down, Begin began to explain:

"Do you see that man? He's the Romanian ambassador. I asked him to deliver a letter to Ceaușescu (Romania's Communist head of state). Can you keep a secret? This is all hush-hush." I assured him that my lips were sealed.

"I'm asking Ceaușescu to meet with me so we can talk about Sadat. I want to know if Sadat can be trusted. Can I negotiate with him? Does he keep his promises? If I get a good report, then this will be the first step toward making peace with Egypt." I did not realize it at the time, but this move represented the inception of the peacemaking process that culminated in the historic Camp David Accords between Israel and Egypt.

Ambassador Kovacs delivered the message and received the green light from Ceauşescu. Begin, along with Alisa, departed for Romania a few days later. While not exactly a secret mission, there was no public announcement made of the trip. The two leaders met on August 28, 1977, at the presidential residence in Shagov, on the outskirts of Bucharest.

Simona and I were still in Israel when Begin and Alisa returned from Romania a few days later, and I met with him shortly thereafter. I listened as Begin shared the details of his encounter with the Romanian dictator.

"After Ceauşescu assured me that Sadat could be trusted, I asked him if he would ask Sadat to come visit us," Begin confided after again swearing me to secrecy. "Sadat will be in Romania in October and Ceauşescu said he would suggest it then."

Begin told me how he reminded the Romanian leader that Israel had years before agreed to pay him $10,000 for every Jewish man, woman, and child he released for immigration to Israel. From this episode, Begin explained, Ceauşescu knew that Israel could be trusted to keep its word. Romania has had direct dealings with Egypt, Begin went on, and therefore was an ideal candidate to serve as a conduit between the two nations which were, at this point, officially still in a state of war.

Begin then went on to describe some of their private conversations on other topics:

"He was always boasting to me about what a wonderful communist economy they have in Romania," Begin said. "He seemed most excited about the latest figures from their state-run shoe factory. He kept bragging about how they had produced 56,659 shoes last year. I was thinking to myself: 'Should I ask him if he's talking about pairs of shoes or single shoes?'" At this, we all burst into laughter.

Begin's back-channel statesmanship succeeded in establishing a diplomatic conduit to Sadat through Ceaușescu. It was through this route that the first tentative peace feelers were transmitted. It would be six months before the first hints of an Israeli-Egyptian rapprochement would be reported in the media. Soon the process picked up steam, and when Sadat's visit to Jerusalem was announced to a surprised world, I was finally able to speak freely and say, "I was there when all this began."

Just as a stop at the prime minister's office was a regular event when Simona and I visited Israel during those years, Begin never failed to get in touch whenever he traveled to the US. We joined him during every visit to America during his term in office. Many times we would meet with Begin at Blair House, where he resided whenever he was invited to the White House to meet with the president.

During the months leading up to the Camp David Accords, Begin participated in numerous one-on-one meetings with American president Jimmy Carter. Oftentimes Begin would be invited to the White House residence for some late night arm-twisting. I recall how a dejected and frustrated Begin returned to Blair House after one of these marathon sessions with Carter. Sessions that Begin had dubbed "nocturnal meetings." I observed as he fell into an armchair looking drained and exhausted. We could see that things were not going well.

"Again he pressured me about Jerusalem," said Begin in a raspy voice. "'Let's talk about Jerusalem.' Over and over. That's all Carter can say." He took a long sip from a water glass and continued.

"But I never hesitated," Begin pronounced proudly. "I told him a hundred times: 'Mr. President, Jerusalem is not negotiable. There is nothing to talk about.' And Carter would say to me: 'You don't have to give me an answer now. Take a few days to think about it and give me an answer later.' But I told him, 'I don't have to think it over. I can give you the answer right now. The answer is the same. Jerusalem is not negotiable.'"

"So how did you make him finally understand," I asked.

"I told him the story of the rabbi from Mainz." This was a Chassidic parable about an eleventh-century Rabbi Amnon from Mainz, Germany, who was the author of the solemn *U'netaneh Tokef* prayer included in the Rosh Hashanah liturgy. Begin reminded us of the tale:

The bishop of Mainz summoned Rabbi Amnon, a well-known Jewish leader, and offered him a job as a government minister on the condition that the rabbi convert to Christianity. The rabbi refused the offer, but the bishop continued to insist and placed great pressure on the rabbi. The rabbi was called back many times, and each time he refused. One time, however, in order to placate him, the rabbi asked the bishop for three days to consider the offer. As soon as he got home, the rabbi became very upset with himself at the terrible mistake he had made. How could he even appear to consider such an offer before G-d? He could not eat or sleep and prayed continuously to G-d for forgiveness. When the three days had elapsed, the bishop sent for the rabbi, but the rabbi refused to come voluntarily. So the bishop had him brought before court by force and demanded a response to his offer. "I should have my tongue cut out for not having refused you immediately." The enraged bishop ordered the rabbi's hands and feet cut off and sent him home. There, the rabbi asked to be brought to the synagogue, where he uttered the words of the famous prayer with his dying breath.

After recounting the fable, a weary, yet prideful Begin looked at us and said: "'I am not like the rabbi of Mainz,' I told Carter. 'I do not need three days to consider the matter. I tell you here and now that Jerusalem is the eternal capital of the Jewish people, and even cutting off my hands and feet will not make me change my position!' I think I made him understand."

Begin developed a deep resentment toward Carter as a result of the constant pressure being exerted upon him. Years later, when both men were out of office and Begin was living in seclusion in Jerusalem, Carter would attempt to meet with him whenever he visited Israel. He would contact Kadishai and ask to see Begin, but Begin would always refuse. With a singular exception, Begin would not even accept telephone calls from Carter because of the unpleasant memories from that period.

Beginning on September 5, 1978, in what came to be known as the Camp David Summit, an agreement was hammered out during a historic thirteen-day negotiating session among Carter, Sadat, and Begin. Simona and I were in Washington when the three leaders departed for Camp David, and no one had any idea how long they would be there. We waited in Washington over the next two weeks and followed the sketchy news reports of their historic activities.

After he emerged, Begin referred to his time at the mountain retreat as "my incarceration." He would complain to Carter, asking him: "How long will we be imprisoned on this mountaintop?"

"I told Carter that I have a friend who was very good at breaking out of prisons," Begin went on. "This fellow became famous for escaping from British prison camps in Palestine, and I'm going to call him up to help me get out of here." He smiled and asked me: "Do you know to whom I was referring?"

"Of course I do, Mar Begin," I responded in schoolboy fashion. "Yaakov Meridor, who else?" Meridor was a member of the Etzel high command and a follower of David Raziel. Meridor was arrested by the British in 1945. They had been directed to his house by the Haganah in a shameful episode that came to be known as the Sehzon (Hunting Season). Meridor was sent to Asmara Prison, from which he made seven unsuccessful escape attempts, finally succeeding on his eighth try. He remained in Europe until Israeli independence had been achieved. He was eventually elected to the Knesset and became a successful shipping tycoon and one of Israel's wealthiest men before his death in 1985.

Briefing us about his experiences at Camp David, Begin went on to describe his numerous chess games against National Security Advisor Zbigniew Brzezinski.

"Who won?" I asked.

"It was a draw," he replied with characteristic diplomacy.

Begin revealed the factor that finally resulted in an agreement being reached. Sadat had threatened to walk out several times during the talks, as had Begin, who even had packed his bags and started loading them into the limo before being called back for yet another meeting. When the discussions seemed to be at an impasse, Carter appeared with some photographs. Both Begin and Sadat had arrived at Camp David bearing pictures of their grandchildren. They both wanted them signed by the other to take home as souvenirs. Carter had rounded up the photos and laid them out before the two leaders.

"It's for them that we're doing this," explained Carter. This emotional appeal evidently succeeded in getting the two sides back to the negotiating table, where an agreement was eventually worked out.

Begin told us how he explained to Carter that, unlike Egypt, Israel is a democracy and therefore the peace accords had to be ratified by the Knesset before Begin was free to sign them. The treaty did not enjoy universal support in Israel. Only 29 of Likud's 43 representatives voted in favor of ratification. Nevertheless, it was finally approved and a signing ceremony was scheduled to take place in the White House Rose Garden on September 17, 1978.

Simona and I were invited to attend the signing ceremony by both the Israeli delegation and the American contingent. The latter invitation was a pleasant surprise since I was, and still am, a registered Republican. When we arrived at the ceremony we noted the large number of prominent Jewish leaders seated with the Americans. While flattered to be included, Simona and I opted to sit with the Israelis. It was a chilly morning as we took our seats while being barraged by the incessant noise of the Palestinian protesters being held at bay by the police.

I recall Begin's impassioned message when it was his turn to speak after the signing ceremony conducted on the White House lawn. Begin never relied upon speechwriters, even when he knew that world attention would be focused upon his words. I can attest to this personally since I was with him on the night before the ceremony as he drafted his speech by hand. Alisa came to us and asked that we lower our voices because Begin was working on his speech for the next day. His remarks were eloquent and impassioned. They concluded with the words: "No more war, no more bloodshed, no more bereavement. Peace unto you, Shalom, Salaam." He delivered this message in English and then, placing a *kipa* (skullcap) on his head, directed his words to the people of Israel as he spoke in Hebrew, quoting from the book of Psalms.

That evening we joined Begin's Israeli entourage on the bus and soon arrived at the official banquet, held inside a huge tent set up outside of the West Wing. Our table was adjacent to the one where Begin, Carter, and Sadat, along with their wives, were seated. We sat with the Speaker of the House, Tip O'Neill, and his wife Millie. Entertainment was provided by soprano diva Leontyne Price and Israeli-born violinists Itzhak Perlman and Pinchas Zukerman.

Begin clearly realized at the time that he was participating in a great historic moment. He recognized the fact that this would be regarded by history as his greatest accomplishment as prime minister, and although we were not together in Oslo, Norway, in December of 1978, when Begin was awarded the Nobel Peace Prize, I am certain that his inspiring words on that occasion also flowed from his own pen as well as from the depths of his heart:

"Peace is the beauty of life. It is sunshine. It is the smile of a child, the love of a mother, the joy of a father, the togetherness of a family. Peace is the advancement of man, the victory of a just cause, the triumph of truth. Peace is all of these and more, and more ..."

A few months after Begin's death in 1992, I was contacted by Kadishai, who informed me that the original handwritten copy of the speech delivered by Begin at the signing ceremony on the White House lawn was going up for auction in Israel. I instructed him to attend as my agent and purchase this precious item ... at any cost. Kadishai was successful, and I held the document in my possession for a number of years. At a certain point, I concluded that it was a significant artifact of Begin's historic legacy and belonged in a museum. Hence, in 2007 I decided to donate it to the Menachem Begin Heritage Center in Jerusalem, where it today is on view to the public.

My donation of this historic item received some press attention in Israel at the time. I might have engaged in a bit of hyperbole when I was asked by an Israeli TV news reporter to explain the significance of this document and I replied with: "I would say that it has the same historic significance in Israel as the Declaration of Independence has in America."

Upon reflection, that might have overstated matters. But I do sincerely believe that these notes, written in Begin's own hand on hotel stationery, may accurately be compared to the famous notes reportedly written on the back of an envelope by Abraham Lincoln as he prepared to deliver the Gettysburg Address.

Yechiel Kadishai was also interviewed by reporters at the time, one of whom asked him how he could be sure of the genuine provenance of this document.

"Very easily," he replied. "I was with the prime minister at the signing ceremony. When he finished writing his speech the night before, he handed me his notes. I folded them lengthwise and stuck the pages in my pocket. Look, you can see. The fold is still there."

On the following pages you will find images of Prime Minister Menachem Begin's personal notes, handwritten on Washington Hilton letterhead, used by Begin when delivering remarks at the Camp David Peace Accords signing ceremony held at the White House, Washington D.C. on September 17, 1978.

Donated to the Menachem Begin Heritage Center, Jerusalem, ISRAEL

THE WASHINGTON HILTON

(1)

Mr. President of the United States of America, Mr. President of the Arab Republic of Egypt, Mr. & Vice President, Mr. Speaker of the House of Representatives, Mr. Speaker of the Knesset, Members of the Cabinets of the United States, of Egypt, of Israel, Members of the Congress and the Knesset, Your Excellencies, Chairman of the Board of Governors of the Jewish Agency, Chairman of the Executive of the Zionist Organization, Distinguished Guests, Ladies and Gentlemen.

"I have come from the land of Israel, the land of Zion and Jerusalem, and here I am, in humility and with pride, as a son of the Jewish people, as one of the generation of the Holocaust and Redemption. The ancient Jewish people gave the world the vision of eternal peace, of universal disarmament, of abolishing the teaching and learning of war. Two prophets, Yeshayahu Ben Amotz and Micha Hamorashti having foreseen the spiritual unity of man under God — will His word coming forth

from Jerusalem — give the nations of the world the following vision expressed

✕ THE WASHINGTON HILTON

(2)

In identical terms:

"And they shall beat their swords into ploughshares and their spears into pruning hooks. Nation shall not lift up sword against nation, neither shall they learn war any more."

Despite the tragedies and disappointments of the past we must never forsake that vision, that human dream, that unshakable faith. Peace is the beauty of life. It is sunshine. It is the smile of a child, the love of a mother, the joy of a father, the togetherness of a family. It is the advancement of man, the victory of a just cause, the triumph of truth. Peace is all of these and now, and more."

These are words I uttered in Oslo, on December 10th 1998 while receiving the second half of the Nobel peace prize — the first half went, and rightly so, to President Sadat — and I took the liberty to repeat them here, also on this momentous, historic occasion.

Connecticut Avenue at Columbia Road, N.W.   Washington, D.C. 20009   202/483-3000

THE WASHINGTON HILTON

(3)

It is great day in the annals of two ancient ~~people~~ nations, Egypt and Israel, whose sons met in ~~our~~ ~~the~~ previous ~~pre~~ times ~~#~~ on the battlefield fighting and falling. Let us turn our hearts to our heroes and pay tribute to their eternal memory; it is thanks to them that we could have reached this day. However, let us not forget that in ancient times our two nations met also in ~~friendship and~~ ~~over~~ alliance. Now we make peace, the corner-stone of cooperation and friendship.

It is a great day in your life, our President of the United States. You have worked so hard, so insistently, so consistently, for this goal; and your labors and your devotion bore God-blessed fruit. ~~Peace~~ Our friend, President Sadat said that you are the "unknown soldier" of the peace-making effort. I agree, but will, as usually, with an amendment. A soldier in the service of peace you are, you are, our President, even, humble dicta,

(4

THE WASHINGTON HILTON

an intresigeant fighter for peace ~~for~~ And ~~Presi~~ Jimmy Carter the President of the United States is not completely unknown. And so is his effort, which will be remembered by generations to come.

It is, of course, a good day in your life, Mr. President of the Arab Republic of Egypt. In the face of adversity and hostility you have demonstrated ~~the~~ *the human* value that can change history: civil courage. A great field ~~commander~~ once said: civil courage is sometimes more difficult to show than military courage. You showed both. But now it is time, for all of us, to show *civil courage* in order to proclaim to our peoples, and to others: no more war, no more bloodshed, no more bereavement — peace unto you, ~~shalom~~ shalom, salaam — for ever.

And it is, ladies and gentlemen, the third greatest day in my

⌖

THE WASHINGTON HILTON

life. The first was day 14/15 1948 when our flag was hoisted, our independence in our ancestors' land was proclaimed, after 1878 years of dispersion, persecution, and physical destruction. We fought for the liberation and won the day. That was spring; such a spring we can never have again.

The second day was when Jerusalem became our city, and our brave, perhaps most hardened soldiers, the persecuted, drenched with tears and kissed the ancient stones of the remnants of the wall destined to protect the chosen place of God's glory. Our hearts wept with them — in remembrance

ימים אשר עשה ה׳ ישמחו בו 14/15 48

This is the third day in my life. I have signed 14/15/79 a treaty of peace, with our neighbors, with Egypt. The heart is full and overflowing.

Connecticut Avenue at Columbia Road, N.W. Washington, D.C. 20009 202/483-3000

to survive the horrors of Nazism and of a Jewish extermination camp,
and some other dangers,

THE WASHINGTON HILTON

God gave me the strength to persevere, to endure, ~~and~~ not to waver in
from my duty
or flinch, to accept abuse from foreigners, and, what is more painful,
from my own people and helpers, from my ~~close~~ friends. This effort
too ~~has~~ cost some friend.

Therefore it is the proper place and appropriate time, to bring back
as a child
to ~~my~~ memory the song and prayer of thanksgiving I learned in the
the home of ~~my~~ father and mother, that doesn't exist any more,
because they were among the six million people, men, women and children,
reddened
who sanctified the Lord's name with their sacred blood, which ~~reddened~~
~~all~~ the rivers of Europe from the Rhein to the Donau, from the
were
Bug to the Volga — because, only because they been Jews,
and because they didn't have a country of them own, neither a valiant
Jewish Army they the offered them, and because, nobody, nobody came to

Connecticut Avenue at Columbia Road, N.W. Washington, D.C. 20009 202/483-3000

THE WASHINGTON HILTON

them were, although they cried out: save us, save us, to the
prejudice, from the depths of the pit and agony; that is the
song of degrees written two millennia and five hundred years ago
when our forefathers returned from their first exile to
Jerusalem, to Zion:

8

THE WASHINGTON HILTON

I will not trouble. Every man whether Jew or Christian or Muslim, can read it in his own language. It is just ~~Book~~ Psalm ~~126~~ one hundred twenty six

Connecticut Avenue at Columbia Road, N.W. Washington, D.C. 20009 202/483-3000

Very few people realize what a price Begin paid for the concessions granted at Camp David. In agreeing to turn over the Sinai settlements, he was giving up his own future retirement community in Yamit, his favorite spot in the entire region. But beyond his personal considerations, he was forced to endure the vilification of the right-wing faction of his own Likud Party. Geulah Cohen, who later broke away from Likud to form the Tehiya Party, rose in the Knesset to denounce Begin as a traitor for signing the Camp David Accords. Begin never forgave her for this outrage.

Over the years, some have maintained that the Camp David Accords paved the way for later agreements such as the Oslo Accords in 1993, the 1994 peace agreement between Israel and Jordan, and the historic Abraham Accords in 2020. I hold a different view.

I feel that the Oslo Accords, negotiated between Yitzhak Rabin, PLO leader Yasser Arafat, and US President Bill Clinton, would never have been agreed to by Begin. He would have sensed the futility of the agreement's centerpiece: the establishment of the Palestinian Authority and granting it administrative autonomy over Judea, Samaria, and Gaza, in the hopes that doing so would, within five years, lead to the establishment of a peaceful Palestinian state. I am certain that Begin would have correctly realized what Clinton and Rabin failed to understand: Signing a treaty that fails to resolve the question of Jerusalem's sovereignty and that does not require both parties to recognize the legitimate territorial rights of the other is doomed to fail. History, I am sad to state, has proven this to be the case.

The utter failure of the Oslo Accords has even been admitted by some of their most zealous advocates at the time. I recall attending a Passover retreat shortly after they had been adopted in 1993. The program included a panel discussion about the Middle East situation that featured acclaimed Jewish theologian and philosopher Yitz Greenberg. Greenberg went to great lengths extolling the virtues of the accords. I disagreed and, when the floor was opened for questions from the audience, I stood up and told him so in no uncertain terms:

"To me, this so-called agreement that they reached in Oslo is a monumental mistake in Jewish history," I stated. "It will never result in peace." Greenberg did not respond to my comment and moved on to the next questioner.

Fast-forward to the fall of 2019 when our family was observing the Sukkoth holiday in Jerusalem. Our host had also invited Yitz Greenberg to have dinner in the sukkah. Although more than a quarter century had elapsed, Greenberg remembered me and my outspoken opinion about the Oslo Accords. He sought me out and said:

"I remember how you said the Oslo agreement with Arafat would not bring about peace. I want you to know that, sorry to say, you were right and I was wrong."

In 2007 the Palestinian Authority lost control of Gaza to the Hamas terrorist organization, which has maintained a perpetual state of hostility against Israel ever since. As of this writing in late 2021, the PA is still being led by the Fatah leader, 86-year-old Abu Mazen, aka Mahmoud Abbas, who is completing the seventeenth year of his four-year term of office and who upholds the PA's "pay for slay" program that provides huge cash incentives for Arab terrorists who attack and murder Israelis.

While the Camp David Accords might well have opened the door to the Jordanian peace agreement, they are, in both spirit and implementation, the antithesis of the flawed and failed Oslo Accords. I likewise believe that Begin would have applauded the forging of the Abraham Accords that were negotiated by Netanyahu and facilitated by the US under the Trump administration—agreements that have already delivered a meaningful peace, based on shared strategic and economic interests, between Israel, the Arab Gulf states, and others.

Whenever I visit the Menachem Begin Heritage Center in Jerusalem, I somehow feel Begin's presence as I look through the photos and memorabilia collected there. I believe that Begin, the peacemaker and Zionist patriot, would be very pleased to look from its windows and observe the newly established United States embassy nearby.

I sense that Begin's spirit abides in the US embassy, a structure that serves to symbolize America's recognition of Jerusalem as Israel's eternal and undivided capital. I likewise feel that Begin would be appalled at the efforts of the current Biden administration to reopen the US consulate in Jerusalem. The consulate was subsumed by the embassy when the embassy opened in 2018. Begin would surely have recognized this push to reopen the consulate for what it is: a blatant act of appeasement and pandering to the Palestinian Authority in the futile hope of bringing them to the negotiating table. As Ronald Reagan often said: "There is no security, no safety, in the appeasement of evil."

Hart N. Hasten

Chapter Twelve

Term Two

As the 1970s drew to a close and as the peace accords forged by Begin and Sadat became part of history, the world watched with anticipation to see what would come next as Begin entered his second term of office. I am thankful that my relationship with the prime minister remained robust during those years. In this chapter, I recount some of the personal highlights of this critical period.

In 1981 Begin was reelected after a surprisingly close race. This time Simona and I were on hand to savor the victory. We watched the returns from our hotel room along with our friends Harry and Freda Hurwitz and Nate and Lil Silver. About one hour after the polls closed, Nate telephoned the prime minister. After a moment, I took the phone and expressed my concern to Begin about the uncertain outcome of the election.

"No, no. You should not be worried at all," he said confidently. "In fact, go call your brother Mark and tell him that I will definitely be forming the next government." His optimism proved warranted since at 2:00 a.m. we were on hand as Begin appeared at Metzudat Ze'ev (Likud Party headquarters in Tel Aviv) and declared victory before a huge crowd of jubilant supporters. Many of the celebrants were Sephardic Jews, members of the Mizrahi community, who had become politically active for the first time in support of Begin's candidacy. *"Begin Melech Yisrael"* (Begin is the king of Israel) was the incessant chant as we pushed our way through the massive throngs of dancing, joyous Sephardic supporters.

Begin, an Ashkenazi Jew, earned the deep respect of Israel's burgeoning Mizrahi community. He accomplished more in behalf of the Sephardim than any other leader in Israel's history, working hard for the elimination of bigotry and discrimination and investing national resources in the development of Israel's poorer neighborhoods. In turn, the Mizrahi community responded warmly to Begin. They loved him and voted for him en masse.

Begin solidified his support among the Mizrahi community during the reelection campaign when he addressed a gathering of Likud supporters where he strongly denounced a controversial Israeli TV personality, Dudu Topaz, who had made an insulting remark targeting the Sephardi minority. The fiery entertainer was exhorting a crowd at a pro-Labor rally held at Tel Aviv's Malchei Yisrael Square (today Rabin Square).

"It's a pleasure to see that there are no *tchach-tchachim* here today," he wisecracked, using an offensive derogatory term for Sephardic Jews. "They always ruin election gatherings like this."

Begin responded to this insult when he addressed the crowd at the Likud rally, which was composed of roughly 50% Sephardim:

"Until today I did not know the meaning of the word *tchach-tchachim.* I understand that the so-called entertainer, Dudu Topaz, used it to insult the members of the Mizrahi community. This is disgusting. This is the type of divisive so-called 'entertainment' our opponents embrace." I recall Yechiel Kadishai verifying the fact that Begin was unfamiliar with the term. "I had to tell him—as we were driving to the rally—what that word meant," he confided not long afterwards.

Simona and I decided to host a victory party to celebrate Begin's reelection a few days afterwards. It was a marvelous affair at the Plaza Hotel in Jerusalem, and every major Israeli political figure was in attendance, including future prime minister Ariel Sharon and the entire Israeli cabinet. We had our five-year-old, Josh, with us and with all the excitement, no one was paying much attention to him. This, despite the fact that many people were aware that he was the prime minister's godson. The guests were focused on the prime minister, who was seated at our table. He stood at his seat to address the crowd and began his remarks by thanking all of his loyal supporters. He then went on to expound on the Ten Commandments as the basis of all human law. Upon concluding, Begin took his seat to resounding applause. Just then, our Josh climbed up onto his godfather's lap and whispered something into his ear. Begin smiled broadly and rose once again, quieting the crowd with his hands.

"My American godson, Yeshayahu Alexander, has just advised me that I should add something when I talk about the Ten Commandments. He says that there should be an eleventh commandment: Thou shalt honor thy children. I agree that this would be a very good addition, don't you?" The crowd roared as Simona and I nearly burst with *nachas* and parental pride. Nobel Peace Prize Laureate Menachem Begin was publicly quoting our five-year-old son on the occasion of the man's reelection as prime minister of Israel. What an indelibly unforgettable moment!

Begin underwent harsh international condemnation when, in 1981, he ordered the Israeli Air Force to bomb the Osirak nuclear reactor under construction in Iraq. Begin relied upon solid intelligence that clearly indicated that Iraq was moving toward employing the reactor in the development of nuclear weapons. It was explained that if Israel were going to destroy it, they had to act quickly, before the reactor went "hot." Attacking it after that point would create a disastrous nuclear hazard to the surrounding area—much like what happened five years later at Chernobyl. Wisely, he opted to act rapidly and decisively. No one, not even his closest advisor, Yechiel Kadishai, knew about the mission in advance.

While Begin bristled at the criticism he endured for what appeared to be an unprovoked attack, he did live long enough to see this decision vindicated during the 1991 Gulf War when Israel's preemptive action ten years earlier was credited—by US military leaders—with impeding Baghdad's drive to acquire a nuclear weapon capability. A capability that would have made Iraq a far more formidable enemy in that conflict.

It is no secret that when it comes to affairs of state, world public opinion holds Israel to a different—some would say "double"—standard of behavior. This was clearly demonstrated when, after the events of September 11, 2001, Western world leaders were urging Israeli Prime Minister Sharon to engage in good faith negotiations with master terrorist Yasser Arafat. At the same time no one was calling on President Bush to sit down with Osama bin Laden to discuss "the legitimate rights of the Islamic people."

Begin ran into this double standard during a state visit to Great Britain in 1979. He had been invited to attend a luncheon at 10 Downing Street hosted by Prime Minister Margaret Thatcher. As an Irgun resistance fighter, Begin had headed the group that had been, to a large degree, responsible for driving the British from Palestine in 1948, often resorting to guerrilla tactics and sabotage. He was labeled a terrorist by the British who had, at one point, placed a £10,000 price on his head. I understood how it now afforded Begin deep satisfaction to be ushered into the highest halls of British power as the representative of a free and democratic Jewish state.

As Begin related the story to me—and as recounted in Yehuda Avner's excellent memoir, *The Prime Ministers* (The Toby Press, 2010)—Begin was seated beside Margaret Thatcher, the British prime minister. Neither brought up the subject of Begin's anti-British past exploits and the conversation remained cordial and low-key. Until the British foreign secretary, Peter Lord Carrington, seated across from Begin, decided to start berating Begin about his government's "intemperate" settlement policies. Begin sprang to respond and met Carrington's criticisms point for point based largely on Begin's profound understanding of Jewish history. Feeling that he was getting nowhere with Carrington, however, Begin turned towards Thatcher.

"Madame Prime Minister," he said with a hard edge to his voice, "your foreign secretary dismisses my country's historic rights and pooh-poohs our vital security needs. So, I shall tell *you* why the settlements are vital. First, Israel is a land redeemed, not a land occupied as the minister claims. Also, without these settlements Israel would be at the mercy of a terrorist Palestinian state. You must understand that we Jews must always protect ourselves. Whenever we are threatened or attacked, we are always alone. You may recall how in 1944 we came begging for our lives—begging at this very door."

"That was during the war when you wanted us to bomb Auschwitz. Correct?" she responded.

"No, Madame, not Auschwitz," Begin corrected her. "We asked you to bomb the railway lines *leading* into Auschwitz. Eichmann, at that point, was transporting a hundred thousand Hungarian Jews to their deaths each week."

Thatcher then dropped a bombshell that left Begin stunned and incredulous.

"You know, Mr. Prime Minister," she said earnestly, "Britain has endured a good deal of criticism over our lack of action to save Jewish lives during the Second World War. I must say, however, that had I been in office and in Churchill's shoes, I would have behaved exactly as he did and refused to bomb the rail lines into the concentration camps. You see, I believe that in wartime one must concentrate on a single objective. Every airplane, every bomb was needed for the war effort. First beat them militarily and then worry about rescue." Begin was shocked and struggled to formulate a response.

"With all due respect, Madame Prime Minister," Begin said, after recovering. "I very much resent what you just told me. You know that by 1944, at a time when the war was surely won and the notorious activities going on at the death camps—such as Auschwitz where 15,000 Jews were being slaughtered daily—were fully known by the Allies, you were sending a thousand bombers a night over Germany. The easiest thing in the world would have been for the RAF to divert fifty or sixty of them over Poland to bomb those rail lines. Disrupting the death machine for only one day would have saved the lives of thousands of our people."

At this point, Carrington interrupted the conversation with a disdainful comment: "And what does all this have to do with the settlements?"

Begin became livid and quickly snapped toward the minister.

"Lord Carrington," he said with a penetrating countenance, "please have the goodness not to interrupt me when I am in the middle of a conversation with your prime minister. Do I have your permission to proceed?" Carrington flushed and fell silent.

After a beat, Prime Minister Thatcher spoke softly to Carrington. "Peter, I believe an apology is called for." After giving the matter some thought, Carrington swallowed and muttered: "Quite right." Thatcher quickly steered the conversation into calmer waters.

"Let's talk about our bilateral trade relations," she said, offering a cheery smile.

During his lifetime Begin was roundly criticized for his decision to launch Operation Peace for Galilee in 1982. Many felt that his regret over this Lebanese military incursion is what sent Begin into seclusion and retirement. I don't agree with this view in any way. I do not believe that the Lebanese War was a mistake, and subsequent events clearly justified my position.

In 1982, Israel was being victimized by repeated acts of terror orchestrated from PLO installations in southern Lebanon. The Lebanese incursion by the IDF that began on June 6 succeeded in neutralizing this threat. The parallels between that scenario and Operation Enduring Freedom, which was waged by the US against terrorist strongholds in Afghanistan in the wake of the attacks on September 11, 2001, are unmistakable. Although the US presence in Afghanistan ended disastrously in August 2021, it did succeed in preventing a repetition of any further 9/11-type attacks for twenty years.

While it is unclear, at this juncture, if the US truly understands how to best address the threat of Islamic terrorism, history has certainly vindicated Begin's foresight and profound understanding of its true nature. An understanding that was, once again, well ahead of its time.

Perhaps Begin's most overlooked achievement was his role in one of history's greatest rescue efforts, known as Operation Moses. Working with then US Vice President George H. W. Bush, Begin sought to provide safe passage to tens of thousands of Ethiopian Jews threatened with starvation and repression in the land where they had lived for centuries. I was with Begin during a key phase of this extraordinary airlift. "I am so proud of our boys," he confided to me with true heartfelt emotion. "We sent our best pilots to Sudan for this mission. They know how to land our planes with no runways over there. They're landing on fields and dirt roads at night and picking up these poor people and bringing them home to us."

Although it became a matter of some controversy, there was never any equivocation in Begin's mind about whether Ethiopian *falashas* were true Jews or not. Their rescue and eventual integration into Israeli society, despite racial and extreme cultural obstacles, served as a shining example of the true mission and unquestionable need for the Jewish state as a safe haven for Jews in jeopardy anywhere on earth. Considering how Israel welcomed the dark-skinned Ethiopians with open arms, I am shocked when I today hear our enemies seek to brand Israel as a "racist and apartheid state."

Begin's second term in office ended in October 1983 when he announced to his cabinet: "I cannot go on any longer" and handed over the reins of government to his old underground comrade, Yitzhak Shamir.

Chapter Thirteen

Fundraising

My time working as a fundraiser in behalf of causes dear to the heart of Menachem Begin encompassed the years before, during, and after his term of office. Whether it was in behalf of Israel Bonds, the Likud Party, or his beloved Tel-Chai Fund, my work was always inspired and informed by Begin's noble and exemplary leadership. In this chapter I recount a few unforgettable episodes that I encountered thanks to my work in the vineyards of philanthropy.

E ven while Begin served as head of state and as a respected world leader, he never forgot his obligations to the widows and orphans of the Irgun fighters. During his terms in office, he continued to raise money for the Tel-Chai Fund in order to pay off the long-standing debts incurred by the Irgun pension fund. Begin would invariably take time out from his busy schedule whenever he visited the US to raise money for Tel-Chai.

During Begin's second term, I was serving as president of Herut Zionists of America and it was my job to identify and contact potential American donors with the means to contribute substantial financial support to our cause. The so-called "heavy hitters." I would schedule private meetings with each donor and the prime minister, who would then solicit a contribution to Tel-Chai. I had asked my predecessor, Eryk Spektor, to suggest some potential supporters in the New York area during one of Begin's visits in the early 1980s. Spektor mentioned that he played cards with an 80-year-old gentleman by the name of Milton Petrie, whom he knew to be a very wealthy philanthropist. Petrie was a mega-successful businessman who owned a major interest in Toys R Us and who had just sold his stake in the Irvine Company for $100 million. Spektor felt that a private meeting between Begin and Petrie, who had recently donated $10 million to the Metropolitan Museum of Art, might result in a $100,000 contribution.

Petrie was delighted when I phoned and asked if he wished to meet the prime minister to talk about an important matter. He agreed to visit with us in Begin's hotel room. After the introductions had been made, Begin explained the need to pay off these long-standing debts in order to preserve the pensions for the Irgun heroes' families. Begin finished the pitch with a plea: "Can you help us with this, Mr. Petrie?" Petrie thought it over for less than ten seconds.

"Mr. Prime Minister," he said slowly. "I'd like to give you a million dollars. Is that okay?"

"Why, of course, Mr. Petrie," replied Begin without showing a hint of surprise.

They exchanged good-byes as I escorted Petrie to the door. Judging from Petrie's bent posture and general appearance, I was none too confident that he would survive long enough to fulfill the generous verbal pledge he had just made. I decided to follow him down the hall clutching a standard pledge form.

"Excuse me, Mr. Petrie," I said as I stopped him. "Would you mind completing this form to document your gift?"

"Young man," he said (I was in my late forties at the time), "you fill it out and I'll sign it." With a quivering hand I wrote $1,000,000 in the box labeled "Amount" and presented it to Petrie. As he signed, he realized that he had no idea who I was.

"There you are," he said. "By the way, who are you, anyway?" I identified myself as the person who had called him earlier to arrange this meeting. I mentioned that I was from Indianapolis.

"Indianapolis? Did you say Indianapolis?" he said, extending a smile. "My father was a policeman in Indianapolis. Do you know the Efroymsons?"

"Of course, Mr. Petrie, I know them well, and Clarence Efroymson has met with the prime minister and has given us support in the past." I went on to point out that I considered Clarence a close friend and had, several years before, invited him to join Menachem Begin at a dinner at our home.

"Be sure to say hello to the Efroymsons and tell them I'm doing fine," Petrie offered.

"I sure will, Mr. Petrie," I assured him. Petrie made good his pledge by giving us appreciated stock in one of his companies. His gift, like that of many others, was not motivated by his support for Begin's party agenda, but rather by his abiding affection for Israel. This fact was demonstrated several years later when Shimon Peres was serving as Israel's prime minister. Petrie also gave him a gift of $1,000,000, telling a reporter at that time: "Well, I gave Begin a million, so I felt I should give Peres a million also."

Another wealthy individual with whom we met during this period was Bill Levitt, the housing developer who had created the famed "Levittown" tract house community in Long Island. Levitt wanted to meet the prime minister in order to express his displeasure over Begin's agreement to give up the Sinai as part of the Camp David Accords. Levitt had invested heavily in oil drilling operations in the Sinai and had lost everything when the area was turned over to Egypt. Levitt and Begin were discussing the situation as the prime minister explained to Levitt about the extreme pressure he faced from US officials such as Secretary of State Cyrus Vance. At this, Levitt, who spoke excellent Yiddish, intoned:

"Mr. Prime Minister, you speak Yiddish, don't you?"

"Yes, of course," Begin replied.

"Well, in my opinion, Cyrus Vance is *Nisht kine über gespitzter* [he's not the sharpest knife in the drawer]. Do you know that word, Mr. Prime Minister? *Über gespitzter?*"

"I certainly do, Mr. Levitt," drawled Begin. "In fact, those happen to be *two* words." They shared a good laugh, and the friction was set aside.

Sometimes large donors would contact me in order to gain an audience with the prime minister. It was during this period that I received a call from Abe Spiegel, whose family had created the Children's Memorial at the Yad Vashem Israeli Holocaust museum. He wanted to meet with the prime minister during Begin's upcoming visit to New York.

"I can try to arrange that, Abe," I told him, "but you must understand that he will solicit funds from you for Tel-Chai, and he will expect you to be generous."

I felt that this warning was in order because I recalled how years before I had met with Spiegel in Los Angeles to solicit funds for the same cause. At that time, I had brought along a true hero of the Israeli revolt against the British, my friend Haim Landau. Landau, whose nom de guerre was Avraham, had been a member of the Etzel High Command and served as its chief of staff.

The solicitation had taken place prior to Begin's becoming prime minister, while he was serving as head of the loyal opposition. In this capacity, MK Begin was able to dispatch a stream of Israeli VIPs to the US to accompany me on my fund-raising junkets on behalf of the Tel-Chai Fund. He had previously sent me General Ariel Sharon (who would become Israel's prime minister in 2001), future US Ambassador Moshe Arens, and others. When Landau and I arrived in LA together, Landau suggested that we contact his old friend, Abe Spiegel.

"Abe is a wealthy and generous fellow and my good friend," said Landau. "I know he'll help us out." Sure enough, when we arrived at Spiegel's office, he greeted us warmly, directing our attention to a photo of himself and Menachem Begin mounted on his wall. After some small talk, I cut to the chase:

"Mr. Spiegel, you know we came here for a purpose," I stated bluntly. "Because of your position in the community, we have come to you first looking for a leadership gift. We have to pay off these debts, and we need to know if you're prepared to help us."

"Of course I am, gentlemen." Spiegel called in his secretary and instructed her: "Please go to the safe and pull out a $1,000 Israel Bond so I can give it to Mr. Landau."

We sat stunned. Landau spoke first. "I traveled 10,000 miles from Israel to see you so you can give me $1,000?! Why are you insulting me like this?"

"Take it or leave it," responded Spiegel. "That's all you're going to get." Landau turned white and then several shades of red. He was beyond anger. "I thought you were our friend," he managed to get out between clenched teeth.

"Take the thousand, Haim, and let's go," I said, standing up. After some further protests from Landau, I took the bond, had Spiegel sign it over to us, and followed Landau as he stormed out of the office in a rage. Once outside I tried to calm him down.

"Haim, take it easy and don't worry about it. We're going to meet some of my friends here in LA, and I know they'll come through." I immediately phoned Bill Weinberg, who was then serving as the chairman of the Israel Bonds Million Dollar Note Society.

"Bill, we're here in LA and I'm with Haim Landau. We'd like to come see you about the Tel-Chai Fund, and we're going to solicit you."

"Come right on over," he said warmly. Arriving at his luxurious Wilshire Boulevard offices, I got quickly to the point:

"Bill, I need some money from you for Tel-Chai."

"How much do you want?" he asked.

"I need $25,000," I shot back.

"If you say you need it, that's good enough for me," he said, pulling out a checkbook and making out the check on the spot. Landau was impressed, and I could see his jaw drop. I could not help teasing Landau a bit afterwards. "You see, Haim. That's the difference between your friends and my friends."

But that all happened years before, and based on that unsatisfying experience with Spiegel, I was hesitant to now book him for a meeting with the prime minister without first getting some assurance that it would be worth the time.

"Don't worry, Hart," Spiegel assured me, "I intend to be very generous indeed. You see, I have a special request for Menachem."

"Special request?" I said. "Menachem?" I thought.

"Yes. I read that Menachem has been invited to travel to Cairo," Spiegel went on, still opting to refer to the prime minister of Israel by his first name. "I would like to accompany him on that trip. And to show you how much this means to me, I'm going to give you guys $50,000." While this was not in the same league as the Petrie gift, it was still a substantial sum and certainly a big step up from the $1,000 gift he had extended the first time we met.

"Look, Abe," I said, "I can't promise you anything, but I will ask the prime minister and see what he says." I met with Begin in his hotel room later that day and told him about Spiegel's request.

"Abe wants to go to Cairo with you, Mar Begin."

"Oh, really?" said Begin.

"And he's prepared to give us $50,000 if you agree to take him," I explained. Begin's reply was quick and definite.

"No. Not for money," he said, shaking his head. "This is not for sale."

"I understand, Mar Begin, but I have a question," I said. "What if Mr. Petrie had said he would only give us the million dollars if you allowed him to go to Cairo. Would you have agreed?"

"Absolutely not, Hart," he said without a second's hesitation. "If something is not for sale, that means it is priceless. I tried to explain this to Carter about Jerusalem. You should not try to buy something that is priceless." I smiled at the comparison and went off to phone Spiegel to tell him that the deal was off. In Begin, I again realized, we were dealing with a highly principled man of unshakable rectitude.

Thanks to our work, and the work of others like Nate Silver, the Tel-Chai Fund was able to negotiate a settlement of all its outstanding debts before Begin left office. This accomplishment provided Begin with a great deal of satisfaction, and he never forgot to express his gratitude for my role in lifting this burden from his shoulders.

Whenever Begin visited the United States as prime minister, Simona and I would travel with him. Begin would introduce us as his close friends to such luminaries as Secretary of State Cyrus Vance, Alexander Haig, and Henry Kissinger. But despite traveling in such rarefied circles, Begin was at all times a very down-to-earth fellow. For example, when we visited him at the prime minister's residence, he would usually invite us upstairs to the living quarters, where we sat around the kitchen table and just "schmoozed" informally with him and Alisa. I recall one such evening quite clearly.

"Another book came out last week about you, Mr. Prime Minister," I commented. "The author made a big deal about how you and Jabotinsky were always quarreling. He says that Jabotinsky was so upset with you that he refused to attend your wedding."

"Ach, such stupidity," exclaimed Alisa, "It so happens that Jabotinsky did attend our wedding. We lost the photos during the war, but of course he was there."

"It's too bad that authors don't check their facts before they write things like that," said Begin. "That's one thing I was always careful about. Every fact I put on paper had to be the truth."

"Speaking of your books, Mar Begin, I was extremely impressed with *White Nights*," I said, referring to his account of his interrogation and conviction at the hands of the Soviets in 1941. He had been arrested for his Zionist activities and was sentenced to eight years of hard labor in Siberia, of which he served a year and a half.

"I thought the book was an outstanding work. In fact, I feel it should be considered a work of literature." I wasn't offering hollow flattery. I truly believed that this book was far better written than anything I had read by Solzhenitsyn on the subject of the Russian gulag.

"You know, it's funny," responded Begin. "My wife also thinks that book is really good literature. And every word in it is absolutely true."

Years later we learned how true this book really was. After the collapse of the Soviet Union in 1991, the contents of secret Kremlin archives became available for the first time to historians and scholars. Menachem Begin's son, Benny, succeeded in obtaining transcripts of the actual sessions during which his father was interrogated by the NKVD. These same interrogations were described, in word-for-word detail, by Begin in *White Nights*. But of course Begin had only his memory to rely upon when authoring the book more than ten years after the events being described. Benny told me that the transcripts and the corresponding accounts from *White Nights* matched precisely, attesting once again to Begin's amazing photographic memory. The transcripts have since been published as an addendum of *White Nights* printed in Israel. They make for fascinating, and frightening, reading.

Sometimes my friendship with Menachem Begin got me into some difficult situations. One such moment occurred in 1982 during the Lebanese War shortly after the massacres at the Sabra and Shatila refugee camps perpetrated by Christian Phalangists. Simona and I were guests at a Bar Mitzvah celebration in Indianapolis. The grandmother of the Bar Mitzvah boy approached me with a stern look on her face. I had met the woman before and knew that she was a Holocaust survivor.

"You're a friend of Menachem Begin's, aren't you?" she said disdainfully. I said that I was.

"Look what he and that General Sharon have done. Isn't it simply awful? Aren't you ashamed?" she was shouting at me at this point, and a small crowd began to gather to see what was going on. I tried to calm her down, but it was impossible to stop her.

"How can you be friendly with such murderers? This is a disgrace and an outrage!" she ranted on contemptuously without letup. I decided that the only way to deal with her was to give it to her straight.

"Lady, let me tell you something" I shot back, confronting her with my face just inches from hers. "I am glad about what happened over there."

"What?" She could not believe her ears.

"That's right, I'm glad," I repeated strenuously. "Do you know why I'm glad? I'm glad because this time the victims were not Jews. Finally, for the first time, we are not reading about Jewish victims. Usually it's the Jews that are being killed either by Christians or by Muslims. But this time, it's a case of Christians killing Muslims."

She stood there with her mouth agape, at a loss for words.

"Don't get me wrong, lady," I said calmly. "I am not happy that innocent people were killed. That is a tragedy no matter who they were. But I am happy that this time they were not Jews." I decided to take the next step.

"As a Holocaust survivor, you should understand my feelings," I said to her. "What about you? Do you ever suffer from feelings of guilt because you survived and those around you were killed?" Her demeanor changed dramatically. A faraway look crossed her face and she spoke softly.

"That's right. I do have such feelings."

"Well, don't you see, that is your problem," I stated. "I know many survivors just like you who suffer from guilt complexes over what happened. Well, I am also a survivor, and I don't have any such guilt. And furthermore, I'm not going permit you to place your feelings of guilt onto me." She stood silently and pondered my words.

"And so, you see, this is a happy day for me," I concluded. "First of all, Jews did not kill anybody. All the killing was done by the Christian Phalangists. And, more importantly, the victims were not Jews, and I am happy about it."

She gave me a resigned look and walked quickly away. This incident clearly illustrated the twisted mentality that was prevalent among Jews prior to the Holocaust. Such Jews are not happy unless other Jews are the victims. If anyone else should happen to be the victim, they become guilt-ridden and uncomfortable.

I recall how Begin expressed puzzlement over this issue at the time. In response to a reporter's question about the massacres, he responded: "I actually don't understand it. The Christians are murdering the Muslims and they're blaming it on the Jews."

An Israeli commission investigating the matter concluded that although they never ordered the attacks, the Israeli military was guilty of indirect culpability for failing to properly control the Phalangist troops under their command. Sharon decided to resign based on the results of their findings.

While Begin's popularity in the US suffered as a result of the Lebanese incursion, he still maintained wide support among the Christian conservative movement. Evangelical Christians respected Begin because of his dedication to biblical teachings and because he behaved like a man devoted to his own faith. It was for this reason that a national ministry known as the Moral Majority announced that they had invited the prime minister to address their annual convention in Dallas during his next visit to America.

It was about two weeks before Begin was scheduled to arrive in the US for what was to be his final visit as prime minister that I received a phone call from, of all people, Norman Lear. Lear, at this time, was perhaps the most successful and celebrated television producer in the country with such popular programs to his credit as *All in the Family*, *Maude*, and *The Jeffersons*. As his fame grew, he, like other Jews in the entertainment industry, sought to use his celebrity as a platform to espouse his liberal political opinions. I was surprised by the call since, like most people, I was familiar with Norman Lear by reputation but I had never met him face-to-face. I was aware that in 1980, Lear had founded an advocacy organization called *People for the American Way* to counter the influence of the Christian right-wing in US politics.

"Mr. Hasten," he began, "I was given your name and phone number by someone who says you are a close personal friend of Prime Minister Begin's. Is that right?"

"Yes," I replied, "I'm pleased to say that is correct."

"Well, I understand that during his upcoming visit to this country he is scheduled to address a large contingent of Evangelical Christians in Dallas."

"Yes, I'm aware of that, Mr. Lear," I said.

"Well, I think it's a terrible idea," said Lear. "I'm sure you understand what these folks are trying to do. Their mission is to convert us Jews to Christianity. I'm sure that the prime minister doesn't understand who these people are or he never would have agreed to it in the first place. You simply must tell your friend to call off this trip right away. I'm sure that if you explained the situation to him, he would agree that he shouldn't go."

"Mr. Lear," I said after a short pause, "you don't know me, but as it turns out, I happen to agree with the prime minister's decision on this matter. These are Christians that love Israel. They have a history of supporting Israel politically and financially. They lobby their congressmen on Israel's behalf. They invest in Israel in a major way through the purchase of Israel Bonds. Many of them travel to Israel and bring needed tourist dollars—even during times of crisis when American Jews refuse to go there. Most importantly, they do not abandon Israel during such times of crisis. In fact, it is when Israel has been threatened in the past that the Christian community has shown its true solidarity by not canceling its missions even when Jewish groups did so. I happen to agree with Begin. These people have shown themselves to be true friends, and Israel does not have that many friends that she can afford to turn her back on any of them."

"I can't believe you're saying that," responded Lear, somewhat taken aback. "Surely you understand that the only reason they are interested in Jewish sovereignty of Jerusalem is for the fulfillment of a prophecy about the second coming of Jesus when all Jews will be baptized as Christians, according to them."

"Who knows, Mr. Lear? Perhaps they're correct," I said good-naturedly. "I, for one, would be pleased if the Messiah showed up. We could ask him that important question: 'Have you been here before?' and get this Christian-Jewish thing settled once and for all."

We bantered back and forth like this for about a half an hour. I believe that I was finally beginning to convince him that the religious questions involved were secondary to the more important issue of Israeli security. I explained that Begin wisely felt that forming an alliance with American Christian conservatives would enhance that security. Once Israel was no longer threatened by its physical enemies, I pointed out to Lear, she could afford to worry about those who would do away with us through cultural assimilation and Christian conversion. Now was not the time for Israel to distance itself from its true friends, such as the Christian Coalition and the Moral Majority.

"When will you be seeing the prime minister next?" asked Lear.

"I'll be in Los Angeles to greet him when he arrives in two weeks." I said that we'd be staying with him at the Century Plaza Hotel.

"Really, Century Plaza? Well, my office is right there in the next building over," said Lear. "I'd like to meet with you again when you're in Los Angeles. Can you come and see me?"

"Certainly, I'd be glad to," I replied.

A few weeks later, after Begin's entourage had arrived and settled in at the hotel, I walked next door and went up to Lear's lavish office, which occupied an entire floor of the modern high-rise structure. He offered me a seat and we immediately began talking right where we had left off on the telephone. But by now, I wanted to know a few things as well. I was hoping to gain Lear's financial support.

"So what about you, Norman?" We were on a first-name basis by now. "What is your connection to Israel?" I had assumed that since he was interested in this matter, he was in some way involved with Israeli affairs. I learned, however, that he had never visited Israel and knew next to nothing about its history and politics. Not only that, he was not knowledgeable at all about basic Zionism. He had no conception that Israel is surrounded by huge enemy nations and that it had been forced to fight five wars to sustain its very survival. I was surprised by this apparent ignorance on the part of TV's "King" Lear. I had met a lot of assimilated American Jews, but for the most part, they had some interest in Israel. In Lear's case I felt that his key concern was being spared the embarrassment of having to explain to his non-Jewish friends what the prime minister of Israel was doing hobnobbing with the likes of Jerry Falwell. I patiently provided him with a basic history lesson, and in the end felt that I had persuaded him.

"You know, that makes a lot of sense, Hart," he admitted toward the end of our hour-and-a-half meeting. Lear agreed to drop his public opposition to the Dallas trip.

As it turned out, Begin never got the chance to go to Dallas because, as related in Chapter Ten, a few days later he was notified of his wife's death and immediately returned to Israel.

Chapter Fourteen

A Leader's Legacy

In this final chapter I attempt to explain the special place that Menachem Begin occupies in the pantheon of Israel's founders and leaders. I also speculate on what Begin would make of the current world situation and offer my assessment—on the thirtieth anniversary of his death—of Begin's enduring legacy.

The fact that Menachem Begin is today regarded by historians as Israel's most accomplished leader does not tell the full story. The list of his achievements certainly reveals Begin's profound impact on history. The Camp David Accords, the Basic Law recognizing a unified Jerusalem as Israel's eternal capital, the extension of Israeli law to the Golan Heights, the rescue of Ethiopian Jews, the destruction of the Iraqi nuclear reactor. All of these and more have certainly cemented Begin's place in the history books. But he is also uniquely ensconced in the hearts of many Israelis—as well as non-Israelis like me. The following story illustrates what I mean.

It was in 1988, several years after Begin had left office, that I arrived in Jerusalem one morning. I had planned to visit Begin at his apartment that afternoon, but as I was unpacking at the Jerusalem Hilton, the phone rang; it was Yechiel Kadishai.

"Hart," Yechiel said, "Menachem would like to see you this morning. Can you come over right away?"

"Of course, Yechiel," I said. I grabbed the books I had brought for him and ran downstairs to grab the first available taxi.

"Take me to the 'Yefe Nof' area, please," I said to the driver. "Once we're there, I'll show you where to drop me off." I did not want give him Begin's exact address. The driver was a bright and engaging Sephardic Jew who, I later learned, was born in Iraq and came to Israel as a child when the Jews of that and most other Arab nations were expelled in 1948. The driver turned around to face me in the backseat and inquired:

"Are you by any chance going to see Menachem Begin?"

"As a matter of fact, I am," I admitted. He seemed impressed.

"Are you *really* going to see Menachem Begin?" he asked again, turning all the way around as his voice wavered with excitement.

"Yes, I really am. Please keep your eyes on the road," I instructed. He complied and then asked: "Could you deliver a message to Menachem Begin from me?" I said I would be glad to.

"Tell him that we miss him so very much. We haven't seen him for such a long time. Tell him that I personally love him so much. Do you realize how much I love him?"

"How much?" I asked.

"I love him more than my own wife!" It was obvious that affection for Begin among Israel's Mizrahi community—a sector that had loyally supported him during his political career—remained very strong.

At this point I got out of the taxi and walked the short distance to Begin's apartment at Tzemach No.1. After greeting and embracing each other, Begin and I sat down in the living room and I immediately brought up the taxi driver.

"Mar Begin, the taxi driver who brought me here today asked me to relay a message to you. He said that he misses you and that he loves you. In fact, he said he loves you more than his own wife." Begin stared at me wide-eyed:

"I hope it's a different kind of love," he quipped. Clearly, Begin's years in seclusion had in no way dulled his lively wit.

This special affection that Begin was able to engender in the hearts of his supporters at times resulted in a type of wistful yearning. I recall my encounter with Bibi (Prime Minister Benjamin Netanyahu) on May 14, 2018, at the formal opening of the US embassy in Jerusalem. Significantly, the date corresponded with the seventieth anniversary of the creation of the modern State of Israel. The embassy move, ordered by the Trump administration as a direct result of the hard work and stringent urging of the US ambassador to Israel, David M. Friedman, signaled America's rightful recognition of Jerusalem as the eternal capital of the Jewish people. As Simona and I sat in our special assigned seats, I noted that with the exception of former Senator Joseph Lieberman, there were no Democrats on hand among the contingent of US dignitaries to mark what was supposed to be a nonpartisan event.

After the ceremony, as I was congratulating many of the assembled Israeli leaders, I was grabbed by Bibi, who knew of my close friendship with his own political mentor, Menachem Begin.

"I wonder," he pondered, "what your friend would have thought of today's events."

"Oh!" I exclaimed. "How I wish he were still here to see this day. I think I know what he would say to you: 'You're very lucky, Mr.

Prime Minister, being able to deal with a great friend of Israel's like Trump. Back in my day, I had to struggle with that Jimmy Carter.'" This elicited a sardonic chuckle from Bibi.

Of all of Trump's pro-Israel measures that Begin would surely have applauded, I feel the one that would have pleased him the most was Trump's recognition of Israeli sovereignty over the Golan Heights. While many considered the Knesset's passage of the Golan Heights Law in December 1981 as an act of annexation, Begin did not use that term. As he said at the time to political opponent Amnon Rubinstein of the Dash Party: "You use the word 'annexation.' I do not." Begin preferred the same terminology used in the 1967 law that extended application of Israeli law to any part of the ancient Land of Israel. In March of 2019, President Trump, at the behest of Israeli Ambassador David M. Friedman, extended US recognition of the Golan as sovereign Israeli territory. I believe this act would have pleased Begin enormously.

I recall, shortly after the passage of the Golan Heights Law, meeting with Ambassador Friedman, who had been highly instrumental in bringing about this measure. My son (and Begin's godson) Josh, who today lives with his family in the Gush Etzion area of the Judean Hills, had joined us. He was brimming with excitement as he unfolded a newly minted map of Israel produced by the US State Department. He directed our attention to the Golan Heights, which now was shown as part of Israel. We both thanked Ambassador Friedman for his role in getting this map properly redrawn, and then Josh pointed to his own community, which sat in an area labeled as the West Bank.

"West Bank? I don't know what that means," Josh joshed. Friedman understood his implication clearly. By pretending not to recognize the West Bank label, Josh was asking when this area, as well, would become part of Israel. Friedman looked at Josh knowingly.

"We're not finished yet," said the ambassador, with just a hint of a smile. Of course, Trump's failure to achieve reelection in 2020 did result in finishing—for the time being—much of the agenda that Friedman had envisioned for strengthening the US-Israeli relationship.

So what would Begin have made of the US administration that took office in January 2021? I am convinced that Begin would be dismayed by the Mideast policies of the Biden administration. As described in an earlier chapter, Begin encountered then Senator Joe Biden during a contentious Senate hearing about US aid to Israel in the early 1980s. At that time, Begin boldly stood up to Biden's threats of cutting off aid by pointing out that he was not a JWTK (a Jew With Trembling Knees).

Begin would no doubt be most dismayed—as am I—by President Biden's support of reopening America's consulate in western Jerusalem. The consulate was subsumed by the US embassy when the embassy was moved to Jerusalem by the Trump administration in 2018. The move was correctly regarded as recognition by the US of Jerusalem as the capital of Israel. Ironically, it is Biden's Jewish secretary of state, Antony Blinken—the stepson of noted Polish-born Holocaust survivor Samuel Pisar—who is pushing for the reopening. A move that would be regarded as an end to such recognition since, according to diplomatic protocol, consulates are only opened in cities other than the capital. I can almost hear Begin's voice proclaiming:

"Jerusalem was the civilized capital of the Jewish people for centuries before there was a Mohammed and before there was a Washington. Jerusalem was King David's capital at a time when only nomads and camels roamed Arabia and Indians and buffaloes roamed America."

When I observe the reaction of Israel's current leadership to Biden and Blinken's plan to reopen the consulate, my heart yearns for a decisive leader like Begin. Instead, we have the spectacle of Israel's current foreign minister, Yair Lapid, timidly saying that the move is merely "a bad idea," instead of declaring to the US, as Begin would surely have done: "Don't do it!"

Begin's legacy can be felt in other aspects of the current Israeli political scene. For example: Israeli Prime Minister Naftali Bennett recently met with Egyptian President Abdul al-Sisi in the Egyptian Red Sea resort of Sharm el-Sheikh. Their talks were centered on security issues involving Iran and Hamas in Gaza, as well as warming up the "cold peace" that has existed between the two nations since the Camp David Accords. This channel would not exist today had it not been for Begin's leadership in forging a rapprochement between the two former enemies.

Of course, the impetus behind Egypt's current interest in improving relations can only be the impact of the Abraham Accords reached in 2020 between Israel and the Gulf State nations. One year in, the numerous economic and security benefits of the accords are becoming increasingly apparent and hence, attractive to other Arab nations such as Egypt and Jordan. I can only speculate as to what Begin's reaction would have been to these historic agreements, but I am certain they would have made him very, very happy. And what would have made him the happiest is that these agreements were reached as the result of strength and not appeasement. They were reached because both the Israeli and the US governments exuded a quality that in Hebrew is known as *yashar*, which translates as an upright or straightforward person. It was this quality that Begin admired and that likewise characterized the man himself. Begin always rejected the concept that "we give the enemy our land in exchange for peace," a notion that he equated with extortion. His motto was invariably "Peace for peace, not land for peace." Begin would have found the idea that the Abraham Accords were reached thanks to a commonality of economic and security interests to be very appealing. He certainly would have applauded the recent exchange of ambassadors between Israel and the nations of Bahrain and Morocco as well as Prime Minister Bennet's recent state visit to the UAE.

In light of his policy of "no land for peace," some have questioned Begin's willingness to give up control of the Sinai, which he agreed to do as part of the Camp David Accords. In fact, the Lubavitcher Rebbe, Menachem Mendel Schneerson, raised this very question with Begin. But, as Begin explained, he never considered the Sinai as falling within the borders of the ancient Land of Israel.

When Menachem Begin was elected prime minister in 1977, the Labor Party was so shocked they labeled the event a *mahapach*, which is stronger than merely a political upset. The term translates as a "turnaround" or "upheaval." But that event was nothing compared to the truly extreme upheaval the world is experiencing today. As Begin presciently predicted when he opposed the Labor government's acceptance of German reparation payments, such misguided acts of acquiescence contributed to the increasing levels of anti-Jewish hatred running rampant today.

We see global antisemitism on the rise at a level not witnessed since the dark days of the Holocaust. We see the American people elect a senile incompetent like Joe Biden to the presidency. That is a true *mahapach*. In Israel they had four elections in two years before they could form a government. Now that is an unprecedented upheaval. And, of course, COVID-19 has turned the world on its head like no one could have possibly anticipated.

As I write these words in the King David Hotel in Jerusalem, as we prepare for the Jewish new year of 5782, I cannot help but observe that I am one of the very few Americans visiting Israel. This saddens me and prompts me to yearn for the days when my hero and friend, Menachem Begin, was leading the Israeli government.

My most salient memory among all the wisdom that Menachem Begin bestowed upon me was the advice offered when I was serving as president of Herut Zionists of America in the 1980s. I was zealous in my efforts to upgrade and expand the organization. For example, I had succeeded in gaining it membership into the prestigious Conference of Presidents of Major American Jewish Organizations. The expense associated with this move met resistance from the religious faction within our organization. I responded aggressively, accusing them of being shortsighted. Begin contacted me and urged me to temper my passion with the words "Don't be so harsh."

You can never be certain as to what aspects of your personality will be remembered after your departure from this world. I find it noteworthy and ironic that this message—"Don't be so harsh"—are the enduring words that I cherish from a leader known for his pugnacious personality some thirty years after his death.

Thank you for joining me on this journey through some of the memorable moments from my friendship with a man I consider to be one of the greatest leaders in the history of the Jewish people. I hope you found it edifying and enjoyable. And so, I close with the timeless words of King Solomon from the book of Ecclesiastes (1:4):

"A generation goes and a generation comes, but the earth endures forever."

דּוֹר הֹלֵךְ וְדוֹר בָּא וְהָאָרֶץ לְעוֹלָם עֹמָדֶת:
Kohelet 1:4

Hart N. Hasten

Photo Album

Israeli opposition leader and future Prime Minister Menachem Begin addressing a group in our home in Indianapolis.

With Menachem Begin at our son, Josh's bris in Indianapolis. March 1, 1976.

173

At our son Josh's bris in Indianapolis. March 1, 1976

(l-r) Rabbi Chaim Ginzberg, me, the sandak, Menachem Begin; the mohel, Michael Aronson.

With the grandmothers
(l-r) My mother-in-law, Miriam Braunstein; Menachem Begin; my mother, Hannah Hasten.

(l-r) Sandak Menachem Begin holding baby; my mother, Hannah Hastern; my brother-in-law, Ernie Braunstein; Rabbi Chaim Ginzburg.

Menachem Begin visits the Hebrew Academy of Indianapolis

The Hasten Hebrew Academy • Indianapolis, Indiana

Treasured keepsake*. An inscribed official photo of Menachem Begin, Prime Minister of the State of Israel. August, 1980*

Simona and me with the newly-elected Prime Minister of Israel.

With Simon and Cyla Wiesenthal and Simona.

(l-r) Me with Ya'akov Meridor, Menachem Begin, publisher Hank Greenspan, and my late brother Mark Hasten.

With Israeli politician, Yosef Burg.

With Israeli president, Chaim Herzog in 1984 . Herzog was the father of current Israeli president, Isaac "Bougie" Herzog..

(l-r) U.N. Ambassador and future Prime Minister, Benjamin Netanyahu with Simona and me during a visit to Indianapolis.

At a 1977 Israel Bond gala held at the Waldorf-Astoria in NYC. Circled, left to right, are Yechiel Kadishai, Alisa Begin, and Bambi Kadishai, as we listen to newly-elected Israeli Prime Minister, Menachem Begin.

Simona and me with Prime Minister Begin at a UJA banquet in New York City.

The Jabotinsky Centennial Medal present to me and 99 supporters of Israel by Prime Minister Menachem Begin. October, 1980.

The Jabotinsky Centennial Medal

is herewith conferred upon

Hart N. Hasten

for distinguished service to the
State of Israel and the Jewish People.

New York City
3 Kislev 5741
November 11, 1980

MENACHEM BEGIN
Prime Minister of Israel

*Prime Minister
Begin congratu-
lating me after
my receipt of the
Jabotinsky
Medal.*

*Prime Minister
Menachem Begin
with his daughter,
Hasia and my
wife, Simona.*

With the Prime Minister in his office.

Singing Hatikvah with Alisa and Menachem Begin.

With Israel's ambassador to the US, Moshe Arens.

With Menachem Begin's son, Ze'ev Binjamin (Benny) Begin.

A family visit to the Prime Minister's office.
(l-r) Our daughter, Renée; my wife, Simona; our son and the Prime Minister's godson, Joshua Hasten; Prime Minister Begin; me; and our son, Bernard.

Prime Minister Menachem Begin in his office with his godson, Joshua Hasten.

Prime Minister Begin delivering his final address before leaving office on the occasion of his 70th birthday.
The Chagall Hall of the Israeli Knesset in Jerusalem. August, 1983.

With Menachem Begin, David Hermelin and Yehuda Halevy, introducing Menachem Begin prior to his final address as Prime Minister in the Chagall Hall of the Israeli Knesset.

With Prime Minister Yitzhak Shamir and Eryk Spektor, former president of Herut Zionists of America.

(l-r) With my daughter, Renée Halevy; Prime Minister Yitzhak Shamir; and my son, Bernard Hasten.

With Prime Minister Yitzhak Shamir, UN Ambassador Benjamin Netanyahu and Freda and Harry Hurwitz.

*Presenting Israeli Prime Minister, Arik Sharon with a newly-published copy of my 2002 memoir book, **I Shall Not Die!***

With Yechiel Kadishai and Tel Aviv mayor, Roni Milo

(l-r) Yechiel Kadishai and his wife, Bambi with Simona and me.

(l-r) Egyptian president, Anwar El-Sadat; U.S. president, Jimmy Carter; Israeli Prime Minister, Menachem Begin at the Camp David Accords signing ceremony at the White House. Washington, D.C. September 17, 1978.

Chatting with US Ambassador to Israel, David M. Friedman and Vice President, Mike Pence at the 2018 AIPAC Policy Conference. Washington, DC.

The Lubavitcher Rebbe, Menachem Mendel Schneerson with Menachem Begin during Begin's first visit to the U.S. as Prime Minister of Israel. Brooklyn, New York. July, 1977.

191

My heroes.
With newly-elected Prime Minister, Menachem Begin and Ya'akov Meridor. The two Irgun Zvai Leumi commanders.

Acknowledgements

I would like to express my sincere thanks to the following individuals and institutions without whose vital assistance this book could not have been produced:

The Menachem Begin Heritage Center

Rabbi Shlomo Riskin

My son, Joshua Hasten

Jennifer Cohen and the Indiana Jewish Post & Opinion

Dr. Jack Cotlar

My collaborator, editor and publisher, Peter Weisz

About the Author

Hart N. Hasten was born in 1931 and is a post-war American Jewish phenomenon. As one of the sole survivors of his boyhood Polish shtetl, he arrived in the US as a refugee and overcame the odds to forge a new life of unparalleled success in the business arena and as an internationally respected Jewish communal leader. An insider within the Israeli political power structure, Mr. Hasten enjoyed a twenty-five year intimate friendship with his mentor, Commander of the Irgun Tzvai Leumi, Nobel Prize Laureate, statesman and Prime Minister, Menachem Begin. Among his many accomplishments, Mr. Hasten is the founder of the Hasten Hebrew Academy and the former president of Herut Zionists of America.

Mr. Hasten is retired after having served as Chairman of Hasten Bancshares. He and his wife, Simona, live in Indianapolis and Jerusalem, and are proud parents, grandparents and great-grandparents.